It Can Happen Here

Jack London
Sinclair Lewis
Philip Roth

Claire Sprague

Chippewa Books
Box 1205
Provincetown, MA 02657

chippewabooks@gmail.com

2013

Cover Photo by Radu Luca

Copyright © 2013 by Claire Sprague

All rights reserved.

ISBN: 1479380202
ISBN-13: 9781479380206

Acknowledgments

Like all writers, I am indebted to many people. Let me single out Jackie Kelly, my editor and my friend, whose insights, patience, and skills were exceptional. Also JoAnn Heiser for her perfect eye and ready hand. And Radu Luca who saw me through many computer crises, including a lightning strike.

Then there are those who listened and were brave enough to say no as well as yes: Irving Schneider, Zola Schneider, Myrna Harrison, Michael Schwartz, Stephen Borkowski, Ruth Kaye, Arthur Ganz, Peggy Prichett, Aleta Davies, Karen Hartnett, Taylor Polites, Sandi Cooper, Annessa Kaufman and Jesse Sprague. Finally, my thanks to the staff of the Provincetown Public Library, especially to Tom Ruane, who managed to get sometimes arcane materials to me from afar with unfailing good humor and success.

For Alden and Jalen

Who Are The Future

Contents

Utopias and their Discontents 1

History as Apocalypse
Jack London, *The Iron Heel* (1908) 13

"'The Hell It Can't'"
Sinclair Lewis, *It Can't Happen Here* (1936) 43

"History Happens to Everybody"
Philip Roth, *The Plot Against America* (2004) 67

Afterword.. 93

Appendix
George Orwell Reads Jack London (1908) 101

References 109

Utopias and their Discontents

Utopias and their opposites have a long history. Even American dystopias, the last of the lot, remind us of past explorations into good and bad societies. When Thomas More (1478–1535) coined the word *utopia* in the sixteenth century in his *Utopia* (1516), he fixed for us an idea whose origins go too far back to trace. I see the Garden of Eden—and More might agree with me—as one of the earliest representations of utopia. Edenic features turn up again and again in modern utopias, which are often emphatically green, peaceful, and without disease, hunger, or class structure. The Eden we know from Genesis projects a myth of origins common to Jewish, Christian, and Moslem tradition. It is also where its opposite begins, where its human couple falls from innocence into experience after their dramatic and controversial interaction. Like Utopia, Eden has become a generic word for many kinds of perfection. The word *paradise*, applied to an Eden seemingly so culturally specific to Judaism, in fact comes from the Persian, meaning simply a walled garden. Its etymology is not insignificant, as it suggests that many cultures interacted then, as they have always done, and continue to do so today.

Utopia and *Eden* remain irresistible terms for the many forms of the good society that have been imagined over the centuries. No one has yet come up with a word as good as *utopia* for its opposite. Neither *dystopia* nor *anti-utopia* nor *counter-utopia* does it. Whatever we call the bad place, it has existed at least as long as the Book of Revelation, which dramatizes the end of the world in unparalleled destruction precipitated by human failures. Utopia and dystopia, these opposites are, of course, intimately related. Both are critiques of the present or, as Terry Eagleton so neatly puts it, "The point is not to go elsewhere, but to use elsewhere as a reflection on where you are" (33).

The two faces of utopia are embedded in the word itself. More changed the Greek *eu*, meaning no, to the Latin form *u* and kept the Greek *topos*, meaning place. But, as the poet laureate of More's *Utopia* points out, *eu*, the same sound as *u* with a different spelling, also means good or ideal in Greek. So More slyly and lightly reveals his awareness of the double meaning of *utopia* as both a nowhere and an ideal place. Or perhaps not.[1] For More's work presents us with ironies we do not always get, partly because the politics of that time are not immediately apparent today, but it is clear that More does not mean to present us with a perfect society. Even more important, his no-place, like all works in the utopian or dystopian mode, is meant as a critique of his own time—sixteenth century England—just as much as Plato's description of ancient Athens in the *Critias* and *Timaeus* is meant as a critique of the Periclean Athens he lived in. That we now idealize Plato's Athens is a historical irony. The story of Atlantis, as Plato tells it, represents another historical irony: that story is, in fact, cautionary. It warns us against the hubris of Atlantis, which became imperial and expansionist and finally defeated by an earlier Athens. Its destruction by earthquake and floods (perhaps by what we would today call a tsunami) is a punishment. Once Atlantis, like Athens, was great and just. In a later period, Rome was similarly to look back at a glorious ancient past from which it had fallen away. Once it too was great and just. These good societies existed in the past as forms of the Golden Age. Literary utopias more frequently

---

[1] B. F. Skinner has this take on *eu* and *u*: "The Greek root ... denotes a place, but the prefix means either good or nonexistent—or possibly, and cynically, both" (30).

look ahead to the future. To locate a utopia in the present time, as More does, is rare.

Utopias can serve comic as well as catastrophic ends. Indeed, what others call dystopia, as one critic astutely observes, is a version of satire or parody (Frye). Comic attacks on utopia occur early in literary history. Aristophanes, another Periclean Greek, parodied Utopia as Cloud-Cuckoo-Land in *The Birds* (414 BC). With the help of the birds, his characters build their city in air. In that impossible endeavor, a contemporary audience would have seen a clear criticism of the Athenian expedition against Sicily. The medieval land of Cokayne, where all things are abundant and free to everyone, is as much wish fulfillment as parody. Its gluttony and ribaldry seem but a faint foretaste of François Rabelais' *Gargantua and Pantagruel* (1532, 1534), an exuberant critique of French life in More's own century. Like More, Rabelais (?1491–1553), a Franciscan, then a Benedictine, and finally a physician, absorbed the humanist learning of his day. In the Abbey of Thélème, Rabelais creates a utopia at once serious and satiric that displays his great learning and irrepressible powers of invention.

Enough. These examples are indeed enough to show how easily utopias can engage us, as I was engaged many years ago when I first read Lewis Mumford's *The Story of Utopias* (1922). I once considered writing about American examples from *Typee* (1846), Melville's life among "savages," and *The Blithedale Romance* (1852), Hawthorne's novel about a commune considered finally dystopic by its protagonist, to Marge Piercy's both dystopic and utopic *Woman on the Edge of Time* (1976) and other more recent novels.

To look back from dystopias that imagine a fascist America to the early European encounters with the Americas is profoundly shocking. For the Americas were then considered an uncorrupted New World, an Eden promising new beginnings. Miranda's exclamation, "O brave new world" in Shakespeare's *The Tempest*, however often it has been used or misused, still radiates the freshness and excitement of the time.[2] Place names like New Hope, New Canaan, New-ark, New-found-land, New Haven, whether Biblical in origin or not, reflect that heady belief in possibility.

---

[2] Aldous Huxley knew the power of the phrase when he turned it on its head in his *Brave New World* (1932) where pleasure and abundance have a grim price visible only to the reader and a few misfits. Leo Marx devotes an entire chapter to *The Tempest* and its relation to the American pastoral ideal (see chapter 2, "Shakespeare's American Fable"). For a more complicated and less idealized historical view of the earlier colonial years, see Bailyn, *The Barbarous Years*.

It Can Happen Here

To recapture the visual impact of this new world on Europeans, there is no better place to start than with John James Audubon (1785–1851), who felt, from a very early age, "an intimacy" with birds "bordering on frenzy" (Rhodes, 22). He used that fine frenzy to produce remarkable engravings of many hundreds of birds in *The Birds of North America* (1827–1838), identifying in the process twenty-five new species. New species, yes, but in his world of plenitude, species decline and species extinction were not yet serious concerns. An outsize personality of exceptional stamina and curiosity, Audubon traveled widely with gun and paint-box, developing many skills, including specimen preparation and taxidermy. He spoke of Native Americans as "man naked from His hand and yet free from acquired sorrow" (Rhodes, 166).

Audubon had a remarkable forebear: naturalist, artist and proto-anthropologist William Bartram (1739–1823), who traveled through what today are eight southern states, collecting seeds, roots, and plants, observing animals, and engaging with many tribes–Choctaw, Chickasaw, Seminole, Cherokee, and Creek. His radical observations about Native Americans come from direct, extended experience. He commented in his *Travels* (1791), for example, that "as moral men they certainly stand in no need of European civilization," which is not the same as saying that Native Americans are "noble savages."

Some might prefer to look at paintings by the Hudson River School for a sense of the majesty and grandeur of the New World. The paintings are fabulous but terribly "literary," tainted with grandiosity, as the works of Bartram and Audubon are not. They tend to embrace allegory. Works like Thomas Cole's (1801–1848) "The Voyage of Life" or "The Course of Empire" were done on outsize canvases of fifty-two by seventy-eight inches, which are more elephantine than Audubon's double elephant folios (at thirty-nine by twenty-seven inches).

The euphoria surrounding the New World and its inhabitants was bound to dissipate if not eventually to disappear, but the idea of utopia had not yet reached its apogee. That was to come in the later nineteenth century.

Like the Americas, the later nineteenth century has a special place in the history of utopian literature. More fictional utopias were written in the nineteenth century than at any other time in history. More utopian communities were also founded than at any other time in history. It was a time when to think the good society was to try to create it—and, of course, to name it appropriately. Consider New Harmony, Indiana: When Robert Owen, the English Socialist, bought it from the Moravians who founded it, he wisely chose not to change its name. That name, so redolent of utopian goals, must have pleased him. Not all the names of the communitarian societies spoke so clearly to their mission. The poets Samuel Taylor Coleridge and Robert Southey were enchanted with a most inharmoniously named Pantisocratic community they hoped to establish on the banks of the Susquehanna. They never got to those banks. But many others found their way to a New World still enticing, although older and corrupted from its more pristine natural state before Europeans colonized it. Some one thousand communes were founded in America during the nineteenth century. Books like *Looking Backward: 2000–1887* (1888) were wildly popular; its sales were second only to those of *Uncle Tom's Cabin* (1851). But by the end of the century, social possibilities had darkened perceptibly under the pressures of industrialism, imperialism, war, and immigration.

The savage reversals of the utopian dream that litter twentieth-century fiction effectively begin with

H. G. Wells.[3] Writing as a committed Socialist on the cusp of the twentieth century, Wells might be expected to hail the ideal socialist future. Not so. In a time when progress was taken for granted, Wells writes against both the grain of his time and his own Socialist convictions about an ultimately better society. In *When the Sleeper Wakes* (1899), for example, the future is not socialist but more repressive and rigidly stratified than any known society. In *The Time Machine* (1895), Wells imagines a two-class system of strange creatures we prefer not to recognize as ourselves. The upper class has become Eloi, the working class Morlocks. The major irony of this stratified development is that the effete Eloi exist to feed the Morlocks.

The Wellsian metaphor is painfully cautionary. If the twentieth century represents the coming of age of dystopia, then Wells is dystopia's precocious prophet. Is the United States exempt from Wells's grim fables? Not according to Jack London (1876–1916), Sinclair Lewis (1885–1951), and Philip Roth (1933–). Wells is in the background of their fictions, with one great difference. The three Americans

---

[3] I say "effectively" because Wells was not entirely alone. One other naysayer should be mentioned: Ignatius Donnelly and his *Caesar's Column* (1890).

create men and women like ourselves: here-and-now creatures in here-and-now societies.

These three writers presume to imagine American fascist states that cannot be blamed on alien invaders or alien ideologies. That is a daring assumption. London's work was written in the first decade of the twentieth century, when the United States was a fledgling actor upon the world stage before its participation in either of the two world wars, Lewis's just a few years before WW II, when the US was a major actor, and Roth's in the twenty-first century when it is the dominant actor. The three novels, the first and last published nearly one hundred years apart, reflect great changes in America. In ways not easily quantifiable but frequently long-lasting, writers both mirror and change opinion. They are, like London, Lewis, and Roth, sensitive registers of their society. These three Americans choose to consider a dark potential in American life, a side rarely represented in mainstream political discourse. Despite their great differences from one another, the three nay-sayers share an unsettling vision of malignant realities beneath American democratic rhetoric. The world once considered a new Eden by its European colonizers has become, in their works, its rapacious, dictatorial opposite. In all three novels, it *does* happen here.

Jack London
The Iron Heel (1908)

The socialist utopias of the nineteenth century were not an attack on America but on capitalism. There is a distinction. Edward Bellamy's remarkably popular *Looking Backward: 2000–1887* (1888), for example, does not particularly target America. Like other benign critiques of capitalism, it expects the transition to socialism to be peaceful. But critique turns to vitriol in the first American dystopia of the twentieth century, Jack London's *The Iron Heel* (1908). In that novel the transformation of the American Eden into its opposite is complete. London's earlier novels, still in print and still widely read, had titles like *The Call of the Wild* (1903) and *White Fang* (1906) which sound like boys' adventure stories. Hardly the likely predecessors for a novel that imagines a proto-fascist America.

It Can Happen Here

London's origins are as unlikely as his literary pedigree. His class background was wrong. The place he came from was wrong. He could have said of his birthplace what Robert Frost was to say of it: "'I know San Francisco like my own face. It's where I came from, the first place I really knew'" (Parini 3). Frost (1874–1963), two years older than London (1876–1916), consciously remade himself as a New Englander. London remained as ardent a Californian as he was a Socialist. He had little formal schooling and much old-fashioned adventure. When he returned at age seventeen from a seven-month voyage to Japan on a sealer, he was sure he would rage "through life without end like one of Nietzsche's *blond beasts*, lustfully roving and conquering by sheer superiority and strength" ("How I Became a Socialist" 58). London seemed like the animals he wrote about. He was perhaps never that and, of course, always more than that. Shortly after turning eighteen, he reversed the familiar trek westward of American frontier myth when he tramped across the country to the east coast, where most literary Americans had begun. What he discovered about working lives turned him around. Getting arrested and jailed as a vagrant was part of his continuing unorthodox education. He did try formal education, but after one year at Oakland High School and one at Berkeley, he returned to his self-education.

Jack London The Iron Heel (1908)

Socialism and writing were early and durable passions. His many jobs—at a cannery, a power plant, a jute mill, as an oyster pirate, and a prospector in the Klondike gold fields—fed both of these passions, as did his later runs on the Socialist ticket for mayor of Oakland and his reporting of the Russo-Japanese War and the Mexican Revolution. He was on the move, writing and traveling throughout his life, even when his body began to fail him.

Compared to Frost, Jack London had only half a career. He died at forty, before the United States entered the Great War (now known as World War I), and before the Bolshevik Revolution, the Great Depression, the Second World War, and the atomic bomb—all these cataclysmic events would have been grist for his particular mill. Robert Frost lived through these events as did his exact contemporary, Gertrude Stein (1874–1946). As it happens, Stein had also lived in the Oakland and San Francisco area (1880–1892) and even attended the same high school as London. But she remade herself away from both the West Coast and the East Coast as an American expatriate in Paris. To even think of Frost, Stein, and London together presents us with a very odd and yet a very stimulating triumvirate. Frost, Stein, and London: their startling differences from one another—the first seemingly so traditional, the second so experimental her work still eludes most readers, and all three so idiosyncratic—suggest a background without tradition, one more Western than Eastern.

In *The Iron Heel,* Jack London's war of the worlds is class war, not alien invasion. London rejects the possibility of a peaceful transition from capitalism to socialism. London's political consciousness is far more radical. For him, only armed revolution can effect a system change. London gives the name Oligarchy to his proto-fascist government that will not surrender power without warfare. Its members are quite unlike the Wellsian Eloi. They are more like George Orwell's Inner Party members, who should be very different from the capitalist Oligarchs but aren't. The reference to Orwell is not capricious. Orwell knew *The Iron Heel*.[1] He had reviewed it and praised it for its insight that capitalism might last far longer than many Socialists imagined, largely because its rulers were so smart and so ruthless. Leon Trotsky had praised it for the same reason. Orwell and Trotsky had the historical advantage of knowing fascism. London's insights precede and have been said to foreshadow fascism.

---
[1] See his "Prophecies of Fascism" and Appendix: "George Orwell Reads Jack London."

Jack London The Iron Heel (1908)

Left luminaries like Orwell and Trotsky, who responded so positively to the politics of *The Iron Heel*, tell us that the novel had a leftist readership. It also had a wider readership (although not one as wide as London had wished for) that has long since declined, while works like *The Call of the Wild* continue to have healthy sales and to spawn movie versions. In *The Iron Heel*, London tried to wed his strong narrative strengths to his early and lasting commitment to socialism. Like Wells, he wanted to write a cautionary tale for his time. He had no interest in depicting life after capitalism. His gut interest was in the apocalyptic armed struggle that precedes the victory of proto-fascism. When he describes that struggle, his great gifts take flight.

If ideology were all, then London might have chosen a simpler narrative pattern. He chooses instead a cunningly complicated narrative structure. Surely he hoped the structure of the novel would make his ideology more compelling. *The Iron Heel* has a double narrative voice and a double time frame. The actual novel uses the manuscript-found-in-a-bottle device long familiar in fiction. A man from the future finds a manuscript written in the past. The man is Anthony Meredith from the year 419 B.O.M. (Brotherhood of Man). The manuscript is by Avis Everhard, wife of the Socialist hero Ernest Everhard,[2] whose diary entries cover the years 1912 to 1932. Meredith annotates his find with copious footnotes that explain the horrors and ironies of early twentieth-century American society. His footnotes are the second layer of narrative.

There are two futures, a near future and a far future. The near future is just a few years beyond London's present time; the far future is seven centuries later. The near future, in which the Oligarchy comes to power, is, of course, the present time. The far future never acquires definition. What little we learn of it comes from Meredith's footnotes. We assume rather than see the end-of-twentieth-century evils in a classless society. London's imaginative lens is wholly on his own time.

For the man from the future, the events of 1912 to 1932 are very ancient history. The Everhard Manuscript about those dreadful years covers the First Revolt, called the Chicago Commune, and the preparations for the Second Revolt, which is doomed to fail and in which Avis presumably loses her life. The manuscript breaks off in midsentence on the eve of the Second Revolt. There

---

[2] Ernest's surname derives from London's aunt, Mary Everard.

will be many more failed revolts and almost constant guerilla warfare before the Oligarchy is overthrown.

Meredith's footnotes provide us with an alternative history of London's America. Appropriately, one of the longest describes John D. Rockefeller, the paradigmatic capitalist who managed to acquire controlling interests in utilities, banking, railroads, oil, coal, steel, copper, lead, shipping, and real estate, an incredible accomplishment no other "robber baron"[3] could match then or perhaps ever can again. Contrapuntal figures like Eugene V. Debs make their appearance. So do some of London's favorite writers: Friedrich Nietszche, Wells, and Oscar Wilde, who fill out the history of our time. Meredith's future knowledge confirms Ernest's unsentimental prediction that under the Oligarchy, unions would become as kept as the press, the universities, the courts, and the state and federal legislatures. Strikebreakers, called "the private soldiers of the capitalists" (129), help advance oligarchic control. There are light moments for the reader who is not living in 419 B.O.M. The footnotes identify Wall Street, for example, as an "ancient street in

---

[3] Matthew Josephson in *The Robber Barons* (1934) popularized this phrase for the creators of the great monopolies.

New York" and regret that no recipe for tamales has come down to Meredith's time.

Meredith the historian judges the Everhard Manuscript harshly. It has for him the expected strengths and weaknesses of participant accounts. He finds Avis's account far too subjective; she permits herself to merge with the events she describes, especially in her adulation of her husband, Ernest. Meredith occasionally corrects her distortions and applauds the immediacy of her accounts. He can, however, also sometimes accept her testimony as definitive, as when he cites her as the authority for giving Ernest credit for coining the phrase *The Iron Heel*[4] for the Oligarchy that was to last three centuries.

The contrasting dual narrative voice is effective. Avis is passionate and partisan; Anthony, cool and objective. One might describe the first voice as feminine, the second as masculine. The novel deploys this established polarity in complicated and contradictory ways, especially in a writer perceived as extravagantly macho. The drama of interacting voices moderates

---

[4] Compare the phrase "the Iron Heel" with O'Brien's image of society in *1984* as "a boot stamping on a human face forever." Compare also Wickson's threat in *The Iron Heel*: "'We shall grind your revolutionists down under our heel, and we shall walk upon your faces'" (63). See Appendix: "George Orwell Reads Jack London."

the sometimes overwhelming doctrinal material that it is Ernest Everhard's role to supply. A novel with Ernest as narrator would have been a disaster.

Avis makes the better narrator.[5] She writes the foreground narrative; she alone surprises us by changing. By the time her journal breaks off, she is an androgynous figure, as much male as she is female. Beginning as a clear sop to romance-reader expectations,[6] this daughter of a university professor—unexposed to socialism, let alone to political thought—becomes Ernest Everhard's primary convert. Avis and Ernest: they are another polarity. She is beautiful and educated; he is overpowering, both physically and intellectually, "a blond beast such as Nietzsche has described" (8). It is not easy to suffer Avis's overheated prose. Still, it must be granted that that kind of prose does not overwhelm the narrative. It subsides almost to a halt when the courtship concludes. In the larger context of the novel, Avis's swooning before Ernest's sexual and intellectual power may be more obligatory than functional. Avis moves easily and firmly to her investigation of an industrial accident that becomes

---

[5] Earle Labor disagrees. For him, Avis is an "unfortunate choice of narrator" (103).

[6] Susan Ward's "Ideology and the Masses: Jack London's *The Iron Heel*" convincingly demonstrates London's indebtedness to popular fiction conventions.

an iconic symbol of the callousness of capitalism. When a worker named Jackson loses his arm at the local Sierra Mills, he becomes an industrial discard. "The case of Jackson's arm" turns Avis from a young woman "swept off my feet" (48) by Ernest's brawn and sexuality into a serious investigative reporter considered "too-forward and self-assertive" (65) by those she interviews. She chooses to learn typing and shorthand so she can become Ernest's secretary: "Our interests became mutual and we worked together and played together" (119). In the world of the novel, this work for her husband makes her kin to the mate-woman ideal London espoused in a letter to his wife Charmian.[7] Whatever the limits of Avis's/London's concept of mutuality between man and woman, at least at this point in the novel the ideal of equality has been stated. It has acquired an existence. Making Avis the narrative voice, the author of the novel, testifies to a greater kind of equality. In *The Iron Heel*, London puts the pen in a woman's hand, as he did not in any other work he wrote.

The Oligarchy's seizure of power separates Avis and Ernest. They are a continent apart, she in one prison, he in another. Their separation triggers the narrative shift from Avis about Ernest to Avis

---

[7] See Charmian London II, 81–83. Also Clarice Stasz.

about Avis. For the rest of the novel, the reader is undercover with Avis. Ernest becomes her partner; rather than she, his. In that undercover world, disguise and disappearance are cleverly linked as weapons of political action. Identity is unstable or "nebulous," to use Avis's word, as befits "the shadow world of secret service"(194). Cloak-and-dagger novels have become commonplace, but the world of the Iron Heel seems a category apart, since in it disguise has become a matter of collective political action. Indeed, cosmetic surgery, then in its infancy, becomes a weapon of the revolution. The art of disguise is very elaborate, going well beyond the nose jobs of our time. It regularly includes skin grafting, hair transplants, changes in body language, in the spoken voice, and even in height. But Ernest knows that beyond physical changes, as he advises Avis in a letter from prison, "One must become so adept as to deceive oneself" (175). Finally, therefore, the most important change is interior. The socialist world of the future, Meredith tells us, has lost the art of disguise because it has no need for it. (He cannot, of course, imagine cosmetic surgery for its own sake.) Avis's "extreme makeover," to borrow the title of a current television show,[8] is so complete, her

---

[8] *Extreme Makeover* first aired in 2002 has been called "the first reality plastic surgery show." *New York Times*, 8.16.07, p. E3, New England Edition.

second self so dominant over her first or "real" self, that Ernest does not recognize her. When he learns the stranger he meets is his wife, he accepts her two selves with humor, calling Avis his harem.

The most powerful testimony to Avis's narrative primacy is London's decision to turn over the three-day reign of terror to her point of view. That reign of terror called the Chicago Commune after the Paris Commune of 1871, an event especially resonant for Socialists as an example of worker governance or perhaps the first dictatorship of the proletariat, had to be set in Chicago. Anthony Meredith describes Chicago as an "industrial inferno" (196, fn. 1) and Avis herself calls it "the storm centre of the conflict between labour and capital, a city of street battles and violent death" (197). London had grown up knowing about the Haymarket Riot of 1886 and the Pullman Strike of 1894, the strike that propelled Eugene V. Debs into Socialist politics. Avis describes her three days in Chicago as her "red baptism" (211), one which forever ends her belief in the possibility of a peaceful evolution to socialism.

The reader knows Ernest Everhard, the novel's ideological center, only through the narrative intervention of Avis and Anthony. His bravura performances before members of the church, big business and small business, and, less formally, with labor representatives, are expository presentations of socialism (London even dares to include a mini-essay on surplus value), presentations that persuade only three people: Avis, her professor father, John Cunningham, and Bishop Morehouse. Ernest runs for Congress and is elected in the Socialist sweep of 1912, but he always warns against trust in parliamentary means. The political left ignores his warnings. Preternaturally suspicious of co-optation, he rejects the offer of the job of US Commissioner of Labor, which Avis thinks is genuine and he sees as a bribe. Of course, Ernest is right. Unions are co-opted, as are elected officials, universities, newspapers, the courts, and every locus of power. The novel justifies what others may see as paranoia. Anthony often undercuts Ernest, who was "not so exceptional as his wife thought him to be" (1), but he does admire his great "social foresight"(142). Thus, only the future in the person of Anthony Meredith will vindicate Ernest's political judgments.

The novel wants to wed ideology and romance, or "politics with glamor" (Auerbach 230). To meet romance/glamor expectations, Ernest must also be highly sexual—and he is. Avis responds to "his splendid shoulders, his two great arms, and ... horseshoer's hands" (55) as well as to "the violence and impetuosity of his love-making" (48).[9] Very physical and very intellectual and very much identified with the working class, Ernest is himself, of course, a version of London. Ernest began his working life at age ten as a millworker, becoming a horseshoer before undertaking a rigorous self-education that includes a mastery of French and German. When Avis meets him, he is a writer and translator and an active Socialist. Some of his working-class credentials have been embroidered, but they are close enough to London's own credentials. Like London, Ernest graduated from blond-beastliness to socialism. Ernest and London have escaped their class but not abandoned it. The novel does become adventure of a special kind that plays out in social struggle rather than prospecting for gold in the Klondike.

What Trotsky and Orwell admire in *The Iron Heel* is its insistence on the Oligarchy's ability to acquire and retain power. London's conception of a self-perpetuating, austere, well-trained ruling class may well have influenced Orwell's creation of the Brotherhood in *1984*. The Oligarchs' "high ethical consciousness" (192) sustains and empowers them. They have been trained to believe that "they alone" maintain "civilisation" (190).

---

[9] "Love-making," the context makes clear, did not mean sexual intercourse.

Jack London The Iron Heel (1908)

Their ethos is important not because no ruling class could be so perfect, but because London refuses to underestimate capitalist power. London keeps the Oligarchy a formidable undifferentiated block force, without a single named individual.

London's reading of violence looks two ways. Ernest always urges his side to resist violence, since their opponents want the left to instigate it. The Oligarchy knows how to foment violence and blame it on the opposition. Ernest knows this tactic very well. At the moment he is felled by the bomb thrown in the House of Representatives in 1913, Ernest can cry out, "It is a plot!" (161), words meant to stifle violent retaliation from the left.

The longest footnote in the novel, longer even than the John D. Rockefeller footnote, is the one that reviews efforts to find the 1913 bomb-thrower. In the novel, as for the Pullman Strike of 1894, the bomber is never discovered, but the striking workers continue to be blamed. London overturns the mainstream view of "labor agitators" as the terrorists of the time and identifies the Oligarchs as the real terrorists.[10]

---

[10] In 1933, the German Reichstag fire was similarly blamed on the Communists. The fire significantly advanced Nazi consolidation of power. There continue to be questions about whether the real culprit or culprits were found.

It Can Happen Here

Not everything that London imagines in the near future is negative. The one great achievement of nonviolence in the novel is the General Strike of 1912, something that has never happened in this country. Precipitated by the government's declaration of war against Germany after Honolulu is bombed, the strike succeeds. A week of silence follows. Nothing runs; nothing works. Remarkably, the strike forces the government to retract its declaration of war. What a dream come true for the Socialists! The election sweep of 1912 follows. This is powerful political romance. From here on, the novel moves swiftly. Its greatest strengths surface when violence begins. The bomb thrown in the House precipitates the Oligarchy's coup d'état that leads to the 1917 Chicago Commune.

Having managed to isolate Chicago from the news that the major planned revolt has been called off, the Oligarchy goes about its massacre of the city with little opposition. The ominous quiet Avis encounters when she first arrives by train from New York very quickly turns into its opposite. She learns how deadly urban warfare is as she watches fleeing civilians and encounters the effects of a new explosive, "expedite," streets piled with the dead, body parts scattered on familiar streets, and people slipping on sidewalks wet with blood. Above her she can see "mid-air fighting between skyscrapers" (212) and air balloons doing what airplanes would later do—dropping bombs. Avis is herself trampled upon and nearly torn apart.

The most monstrous plan, one to herd the working-class population (the privileged neighborhoods are untouched) of the city into Lake Michigan, successfully drowns forty thousand people before it is aborted. Was this plan original to London? There are booby traps everywhere: inside buildings, on rooftops, and in the new automobiles.[11]

With assistance from another double agent, Avis spends the night in an abandoned harness shop (an incongruous image here of a more pastoral pre-machine age). Mercenaries, the troops that developed out of the old Army, battle workers or what London calls, after Wells, "the people of the abyss."[12] (In *1984*,

---

[11] The Model T was introduced in 1906; in 1909, 10,607 were sold. (Zinn 324). Neither London, Lewis, nor Roth is interested in the technological advances common in science fiction. Expedite (an explosive London made up and named), air balloons dropping bombs, and automobiles are as far as London goes.

[12] The term *abyss* was applied to the poor of London's East End. The phrase "people of the abyss" is from Wells's *Anticipations* (1902). London went among the London poor in disguise for his *The People of the Abyss* (1903). Orwell was influenced by London in his disguised descents in *Down and Out in Paris and London* (1933) and *The Road to Wigan Pier* (1937).

they are called proles.) The working class appears leaderless. Double agents like Avis wander dazed, getting by on passwords exchanged with other agents.

Avis insists on Ernest's gentle side. Ernest, the macho activist, espouses nonviolent political action. He understands the allure of violence that Avis has yet to learn. And she does. Her transformation during the Commune explicitly alludes to the Nietzschean transvaluation of values:

> A transformation came over me. The fear of death, for myself and for others, left me.
>
> I was strangely exalted.... Nothing mattered. The Cause for this one time was lost, but the Cause would be here tomorrow, the same Cause, ever fresh and ever burning.... For my mind had leaped to a star-cool attitude and grasped a passionless transvaluation of values (208).

Avis's immersion in violence paradoxically makes her cool and immune to it.

Violence may, finally, be endemic to London's conception of progress. But the hyper-individualism implicit in blond-beastliness is tempered by

Jack London The Iron Heel (1908)

London's political conversion. He knew his youth and strength could not last forever. He also knew, and we need to remember, that Ernest is only one part of himself. London had, in his own life, come "perilously close to the bottom of capitalist society" (Franklin v). To see London/Ernest as only an *ubermensch* is to eliminate everything that made him a Socialist, everything which made him identify with those who could be and were herded into Lake Michigan.

Every utopian novel since More's *Utopia* has been a critique of the writer's own time. What London sees in the near future goes very little beyond what was happening in his own present. But that "little beyond" is crucial. However slight the leap from the capitalism of his time to fascism may seem, to take that leap is a radical act, whether it is taken in the imagination or in fact. As it happens, London's fictional 1912–1932 is frighteningly like what essentially (if not in point-for-point equivalence) was to happen. Both *It Can't Happen Here* and *The Plot Against America* know the trauma of these years. The *Iron Heel* is a wrenching Cassandra cry against the future that could be.

The years 1880–1908 were so economically turbulent that historians have stopped counting the panics of the 1890s and found it easier to refer to the decade as the "Crisis of the 90s" (Williams 21). These crises, continuing right up to the beginning of the Great War, then called "panics," were successively replaced by kinder words: first by *depression,* then by *recession.* Labor violence seemed an inevitable accompaniment of economic instability. The Socialists connected bad times and appalling working conditions with the growth of monopolies. So did many others who, like Ernest Everhard, believed that combination is better than competition. In fact, competition was not as characteristic of the period as was once believed.[13] In the United States (but not in a post-Versailles Europe, where the 1920s were anything but "roaring"), this decade seems in retrospect only a brief respite from a long run of economic ills. In Germany economic turbulence was to lead to the election victory of the Nazi Party in 1933. The Great Depression followed hard upon the end of the 1920s and did not end until the beginning of World War II in 1939. It is not uncommon to describe America's imperial expansion as an answer to the economic disasters of the period, which were exacerbated by the closing of

---

[13] Standard Oil is the major exception. The railroad, steel, and banking industries combined more than they competed. See Kolko, 2–7.

the frontier and the consequent end of westward expansion.

London saw his world self-destructing. He was right, for just six years after the publication of *The Iron Heel,* the Great War officially erupted, and, by its end, two years after Jack London died, a short-lived Spartacist Revolt in Germany failed, but a Socialist revolution in Russia succeeded. It was possible for London to imagine American Socialists nearly coming to power in 1912, but not to imagine that a party he considered politically naive could maintain power. Not surprisingly, London's novel predicts the failure of left parliamentarianism and the success of right-wing armed revolution.

London's world was of course self-destructing all along, as he very well knew. The Great War was preceded by "little" wars. The United States began its imperial expansion in London's time with its own "little" wars in Hawaii, Central America, the Caribbean, and the Pacific. The takeover of Hawaii in 1893, when London was an impressionable seventeen-year-old, didn't even get to be called a war. It all happened too quickly and without casualties. Just five years later, the country acquired not only Cuba but also the faraway Philippines in the Spanish American War, which then Secretary of

It Can Happen Here

State John Hay famously called "a splendid little war." A long string of other "little" wars included the Opium Wars, the Boer War, the Russo Japanese War, and other less "hot" wars over markets in China, Africa, India, and the Americas. Diplomatic, commercial, and missionary interests coincided and colluded. Markets circled the globe long before the airplane did. From London's point of view, both the big and the little wars were imperial wars heading toward open seizure of power at home and overseas

We take the name *fascism* from Benito Mussolini's party, which came to power in Italy in 1922, and *Nazism* from Adolf Hitler's National Socialist Party, which took power in 1933. London would not have been surprised. To someone who knew that the world of global and imperial power had no national borders, imagining a war starting in Honolulu wasn't much of a stretch. The aggressor was different, but the place was the same in 1941. Honolulu turned out to be the right place for the Japanese attack that brought the United States into the Second World War.[14]

---

[14] London's awareness of irony is here in the background. Germany was the aggressor in 1914. It also had strong left-wing parties. Americans knew immigrants were blamed for much of the labor violence in the period. Germany was the original home of most of the eight anarchists considered responsible for the deaths of police and strikers in Haymarket Square.

Jack London The Iron Heel (1908)

War seemed endemic to the twentieth century and may come to be so for the twenty-first as well. To see war and economic disaster continuing from the present into the future did not take special prescience; to see that they could lead to a right-wing takeover in the United States, did.

London's prescience shows in other ways as well. The novel is more than a display of the "superman in red" (Hicks 111). Avis's metamorphosis from adoring wife to revolutionary activist and double agent begins with the bloody Chicago Commune, which one critic likens to Picasso's *Guernica* (Beauchamp 90). Avis's development has been described as evidence of London's "visionary transformation of masculinity and femininity" (Stasz 122). "Visionary" may be strong, but London's portrayal of Avis, "although no feminist's dream," does qualify as "a male chauvinist's nightmare" (Stasz 118). After Ernest's imprisonment, Avis becomes the hero of the novel. Her portrayal forces us to revise older views of London's extreme machismo.

Oligarchic rule brings with it the extreme degradation of the working class. London's "people of the abyss"[15] become the degraded poor, more like

---

[15] See *People of the Abyss* (1903).

helots or serfs. They have no mobility; they can neither change jobs nor where they live. Their old liberties gone, they are imprisoned in "labour-ghettoes." If any worker shows ability, he is co-opted into the Mercenaries, the police force that developed out of the old army and found its own "morality and consciousness" (190). The resemblances between the "people of the abyss" and Orwell's "proles" are striking.

A less remarked insight is London's insistence on the slipperiness of identity in a time of guerrilla warfare under totalitarian rule. Double agents are not the only people to profit from the weapons of disguise and disappearance. Professor Cunningham, Avis's father, and especially Bishop Morehouse learn how to manipulate how they look and where they move about. The professor—fired by his university, his books suppressed, himself forced into homelessness—learns how to live underground under the Oligarchy. Through the character of the bishop, London shows an early awareness of how mental illness can be used to neutralize dissidents. The Bishop's "madness" imprisons him, but he manages to escape again and again, using disguise and disappearance successfully in order to pursue his ministry. The bishop and the professor were lucky. Other people disappeared forever, like the "disappeared" of our time.[16]

It would be hard to say anything worse about *The Iron Heel* than has already been said, including London's own words in a letter to a friend, when he describes the novel as "'a labor of love and a dead failure as a book'" (quoted by Labor 102). It's not clear whether London is describing reviewer judgments or saying what he himself thought. One critic condemns Avis and Ernest as "little more than walking phonographs" and more than half the book as "only an animated pamphlet" (Rideout 445). Even a left-wing reader protested that Ernest is still London's usual superman with red politics (Hicks 191). Other voices are less negative. One even considers it the *1984* of its day (Lerner vii). Trotsky admired the "audacity and independence" (v) of the book's historical foresight; Orwell, the novel's awareness that "hedonistic societies do not endure" (30). They admire the book's politics, but they are less than enthusiastic about the novel as a novel. *The Iron Heel* may not be as good as many would like it to be, but it is better than its worst critics think it is.

---

[16] Anthony Meredith tells the readers of 419 B.O.M: "Disappearance was one of the horrors of the time" (174, fn. 1).

The novel's cunning narrative structure should have worked well. Yet it did not. Perhaps problems of execution, or, as some would have it, ideology, deformed what could have made an excellent dark prophecy. Its power of blackness, to appropriate a phrase Herman Melville used of Nathaniel Hawthorne, is exceptional, particularly in an era considered "confident" by so many.[17]

London's blackness, so wholly secular, has no basis in the Calvinist belief in innate depravity and original sin "from whose visitations," Melville believed, "no deeply thinking mind is always and wholly free" ("Hawthorne's Mosses"). Melville's sense of darkness coexists incongruously with a most optimistic sense of literary, even political, nationalism akin to Whitman's. Melville believes in an "American genius." To encourage that genius, he is willing to applaud even mediocrity. Like Whitman, he longed for an American literature. Not so London, who ignores national identity and literary destiny as thoroughly as he ignores the country's New England literary example. He does, however, share with Henry James (1843–1916) a revulsion against what James called

---

[17] See, for example, Van Wyck Brooks. *The Confident Years, 1880–1915*. Other contrarian literary voices included Ambrose Bierce, the later Mark Twain, and Henry Adams.

Jack London The Iron Heel (1908)

"the huge American rattle of gold" (*The American Scene*, 114). In post–Civil War America, Melville's prose grew darker (e.g., "Bartleby the Scrivener" and "Benito Cereno"). Even Whitman calmed his exuberant literary and political nationalism, lamenting as early as 1867 the American "march with unprecedented strides to empire so colossal." That march to "empire so colossal" meant for him the annexation of "Texas, California, Alaska and [the] reach north for Canada and south for Cuba" (*Democratic Vistas*). By 1908, London knew an American "empire" larger, even without Canada, than Whitman imagined.

The most astonishing omission in *The Iron Heel* has gone unnoticed. The novel shows no awareness of the idea of American promise. To leave that centerpiece of American rhetoric out suggests that its existence was less widespread than many historians and popular rhetoric have assumed. It seems unlikely that London would have deliberately bypassed the idea of American promise or of its extension, American exceptionalism, since either or both overlapping premises would have served his thesis well. Sinclair Lewis and Philip Roth believe in an American promise without imperial coattails. They had expectations to be dashed. London seems to have had none. There is nothing exceptional about London's present-day or past America. It is merely one among many industrial capitalist nations.

The likelihood is that London's socialism insulated him from imperial literary and political baggage.[18] An America with so blank a past and so bleak a future cannot be imagined in earlier American writers. London's particular power of blackness continues to keep *The Iron Heel* alive. Against all odds, it stubbornly survives.

---

[18] I am indebted to Michael Schwartz for this insight.

It Can't Happen Here (1935)

When Sinclair Lewis published *It Can't Happen Here* in 1935, he had already written over a dozen novels and received the Nobel Prize for literature, the first American to be so honored. Most of these novels are not memorable, but five must be counted his best. These five, published between 1920 and 1929, neatly stretch across the decade of the 1920s and continue to undercut superficial judgments of what the twenties were all about. They join the many works of these years that testify to the coming of age of American literature. If the country was experiencing a very special high during the 1920s—the decade has been called "roaring"—that high did not go along with applause for the quality of American life. Writers of the decade like T. S. Eliot, F. Scott Fitzgerald, Ernest Hemingway, John Dos Passos, and Eugene O'Neill were not high on the quality of American life. Perhaps Lewis Mumford and others who thought the Nobel Prize could more properly have been granted elsewhere were right. (Mumford would have preferred Robert Frost.) But Lewis's accomplishment seemed gargantuan then, even if it seems less so now. *Main Street,* "the most sensational event in twentieth century American publishing history" (Schorer 268), opened the decade in 1920; *Babbitt* followed in 1922, *Arrowsmith* in 1925, and *Elmer Gantry* in 1927. Finally *Dodsworth* appeared during the year of the crash, 1929. The list is impressive. Lewis had refused a Pulitzer, but accepted the Nobel in 1930. Some critics undercut the award, believing that Lewis was chosen because his work gave Europeans the America they believed in, one conformist, provincial, materialistic, and shallow. In his acceptance speech, Lewis did not speak to that America. Instead he spoke as one of a different constellation. He did not think of himself as an isolated or exceptional figure. He named older writers like Theodore Dreiser, Willa Cather, and Sherwood Anderson and younger ones like William Faulkner. His Nobel acceptance speech described a more complicated America, one that was both "the most depressing [and] the most stirring of any land in the world today" (Nobel Lecture).

What a charged, even thrilling, moment it must have been for the twenty-year-old Lewis to meet Jack London, another forerunner, a wunderkind really, who managed to achieve great popular success. The two met at Yale, where London had come to speak for socialism, not for literature. It was 1905, and London may not yet even have conceived of *The Iron Heel*. Was the moment of their meeting diluted when London admitted to needing plot ideas? How did the as-yet-unpublished undergraduate think about feeding plot ideas for money to so celebrated a literary hero? Did he feel puffed up? Or did his hero sink in his estimation? The relationship between London and Lewis did not develop.

Perhaps its very insubstantiality raises anew the questions raised in the period about the limits, indeed the aridity of the literary life in America when even writers didn't know how to talk to one another (see, for example, Cowley and Brooks). The London-Lewis interaction, at once so ordinary and so bizarre, remains a tantalizing one. It has no resemblance to Herman Melville's meeting with Nathaniel Hawthorne, which had so strong an impact on Melville.

If Lewis could not learn from London the man, he could learn from London the writer. And he did. *The Iron Heel* is in the background of *It Can't Happen Here*. It was a phenomenon the politically conscious Lewis could not ignore. If native fascism was conceivable to London in 1908, it was even more easily conceivable to Lewis in 1935, when the country was in deep depression, right-wing demagogues were plentiful, and there was a new word, *fascism*, for the kind of social structure London had described as Oligarchy. Lewis's Corpo regime owes more to London than to Italian fascism; one critic describes the Corpo regime as "London's Oligarchy thinly disguised" (Jones 219). Lewis's Corpos are imagined without the austerity and dedication of the Oligarchy.[1] The details of Lewis's indebtedness are less crucial than Lewis's primary indebtedness to London for the shocking postulate that America could go fascist and in the present time, not in some distant future.[2] Like London's novel, Lewis's dramatically overturns the nineteenth-century socialist utopias, typified by *Looking Backward*, in which Bellamy's serene and sensible socialism comes about without violence.

The timing of *It Can't Happen Here* was perfect. In the worldwide depression[3] of the 1930s, the

---

[1] London's Oligarchy is more like Orwell's Brotherhood. See Appendix: "George Orwell Reads Jack London."

[2] See Coard for an extended examination of Lewis and London.

[3] What was so graphically called a "panic" in London's time had euphemistically come to be called a "depression," its later meaning inflamed by an initial capital and the adjective "Great." In the phrase "The Great Depression" that mild word has acquired the power to frighten, ironically overturning its original euphemistic intention. In time another euphemism was required, and it was found in the word *recession*, which is still in vogue.

It Can't Happen Here (1935)

United States and Germany were hit hardest, but the American depression lasted longer. Images of the period are plentiful in this first economic cataclysm to be exploited by the mass media. In movies, newsreels, Sunday color sections, plentiful daily newspapers, popular song, radio, and vaudeville, people saw the breadlines, the migrant farmers, the strikers, the bonus marchers, the apple sellers, and the bank failures. Unemployment ran as high as 25 percent. Not the NRA, the WPA, the CCC, or any other of Franklin D. Roosevelt's projects solved the crisis of capitalism.

Other events had long-term seismic effects. The country was still coming to terms with immigrants who spoke many different languages. In one factory, the local union published leaflets in seven different languages. It took a while for the history books to catch up with the effects of the internal migration of over a million southern African Americans to the north and to consider the effects of that migration together with the European immigrations, but it needed to be. The Sacco and Vanzetti trial and execution seemed to many participants and observers a litmus example of deep-seated prejudice against immigrants, labor, and the left. The case attracted international attention. Americans in Paris reported being warned to stay indoors on the night of the execution in 1927. The Chinese, who, together with the Irish, had been the main labor force for the building of the railroads, were specifically barred from entry into the country. That exclusion was the first legislation to bar a specific ethnic group from entrance to the country. The Chinese Exclusion Acts were on the books for just over sixty years, from 1882 to 1943.

Lewis could not know when he wrote his novel that the depression would not be over until 1939 or that the crisis of capitalism was finally relieved only with the coming of World War II. That eventuality seemed a textbook illustration of Randolph Bourne's incendiary phrasing that "War is the health of the state" (71). His line trumped two major slogans of the Great War—that it would be the war to end all wars and that it would make the world safe for democracy. There were "small" wars before 1935, like the Japanese invasion of Manchuria in 1931 and Mussolini's invasion of Ethiopia in October 1935, the very month the Lewis novel was on the stands. Historical hindsight generally credits the punitive Treaty of Versailles with enabling the rise of Fascism in Italy and Nazism in Germany. Fascism succeeded in Italy only four years after the end of the Great War. Hitler's rise came close to home for Lewis through Dorothy Thompson, his second wife, a well-known

It Can't Happen Here (1935)

journalist who had been tracking Hitler since 1931 and was forbidden from entering Germany in 1934, a year after his election, when hardly anyone considered him a threat. Family talk was heavily political. Lewis is said to have quipped that if ever he divorced, Hitler would be named a co-respondent.

The details of the book's pre-publication history are well known. It was written in only four months, from May to August of 1935, while Lewis and his wife were living in their Vermont summer house, and published in October of the same year.

Lewis opens his novel in May 1936, which means he is telling his readers that in November, after the next election, they will be living in a fascist America. Despite the novel's dire prediction, or perhaps because of it, *It Can't Happen Here* became a best seller. The American electorate was scared and Lewis spoke to its fears. He chose as his setting not the middle west, which he had so satirized in his earlier novels, but the Vermont so strongly associated with liberty and so presumably insulated from middle western shallowness. Perhaps its granite quarries and woolen mills are more to the point in a Vermont that turns out to be as Rotary as Zenith or Gopher Prairie. The opening communal chapter does not treat us to the famed New England town meeting. There is no individualism; there is no democracy in action. The center of town life is the Ladies Night Dinner of the Fort Beulah Rotary Club. The guests are already racist, anti-Semitic, militarist, and jingoist. They need no conversion; they are already Corpos.

Critics generally agree that Lewis's great satiric gifts work through his "packed and brilliant detail" (Mencken, "Consolation," 19). Constance Rourke describes his strength as "highly circumstantial fable-making" of a kind she considers a particularly "American gift for comic mimicry" (30). Others have found his irony and sarcasm "cheap and showy" (Whipple 80). Both positions may be true. The tables spread before the guests include "figurines of Mickey Mouse, brass Rotary wheels and small silk American flags stuck in gilded hard-boiled eggs" (2). Patriotic indeed. The menu proper is similarly grotesque. Some have criticized Lewis's overzealous attention to social detail; E. M. Forster called him a man with a camera, but another critic points out that a camera eye selects (Mumford).

The guests listen to General Herbert Y. Edgeways' "manly yet mystical remarks on nationalism" (2), which introduce the main speaker, Mrs. Adelaide Tarr Gimmitch. The applause is "cyclonic" (3). *Cyclonic*, obviously the author's undercutting word,

It Can't Happen Here (1935)

tells the reader to judge the proceedings negatively. The main speaker, "renowned for her gallant anti-suffrage campaigning" and for keeping "American soldiers out of French cafes by the clever trick of sending them ten thousand sets of dominoes" (1), wants women now to have six children and forgo the vote. The targets and the language are obvious. In fact, the coexistence of such a near-farcical tone with the portrayal of a fascist America is an uneasy one throughout the novel. There are two contrarian voices, one silent and one vocal; one belongs to the protagonist, Doremus Jessup, editor of the Fort Beulah *Daily Informer*, the other to Lorinda Pike, his lover. Doremus inwardly reflects on the irony of Mrs. Gimmitch and her fellow DAR members choosing to pay homage to what were seditious American colonists, while Lorinda asks aloud whether "'a poor gal who can't hook a man … should have her six kids out of wedlock?'" (6). Mrs. Gimmitch replies that a woman "'with any real charm and womanliness'" wouldn't have a problem getting a man (6).

These two sets of voices and the contrarian voices of Doremus and Lorinda are put into play by the author's voice. There are, then, at least three sets of voices in the opening chapter with the reader being manipulated into siding with the author against the Rotarians. The novel is unexpectedly managed in a complex narrative style (McLaughlin 29) "full of contending tongues" (Meisel 11).

In November, Berzilius (Buzz) Windrip (the bad politicos get the comic names) is elected president on the Democratic ticket; Walt Trowbridge, the Republican, comes in second and FDR third on the new Jeffersonian ticket he forms when the Democrats reject him. Doremus had traveled to New York on election eve to hear Buzz speak at Madison Square Garden. What is he really like? Buzz turns out to be a mesmerizing speaker, a shock to Doremus, who was so sure Buzz could be easily dismissed. His planned vote for Trowbridge is even more firm, because only Trowbridge just might defeat Windrip. Like Huey Long (assassinated only months before *It Can't Happen Here* was published), the model for Buzz Windrip, Buzz makes an unbeatable populist presence. He tells himself even near the end of his reign "that his main ambition was to make all citizens healthy, in purse and mind and that if he was brutal it was only toward fools and reactionaries" (340).

The Rasputin, the Karl Rove, if you will, of this "Professional Common Man" (72), as Doremus calls him, is Lee Sarason whose "genius was and remained a mystery" (28). He surfaces early in Windrip's career as the managing editor of a major newspaper when Windrip runs for senator in an unnamed western state. Sarason had been many things, been many places, tried out being a Socialist, even an anarchist, finally believing "only in resolute control by a small oligarchy. In this he was a Hitler, a Mussolini" (29). The word *oligarchy* is another reminder of London, who uses it for his proto-fascist regime in *The Iron Heel*. Sarason is called Windrip's secretary but is "known to be much more—bodyguard, ghost-writer, press-agent, economic adviser" (29). Sarason surely put into written form Windrip's *Zero Hour—Over the Top* from notes provided by Buzz. Considered "the Bible of his followers" (29), *Zero Hour* stands as an obvious analogue to Hitler's *Mein Kampf*. (Epigraphs from *Zero Hour* precede the first twenty chapters.) Jessup and Sarason, both newspapermen, are, however, as unalike, to paraphrase Lewis, as the village parson and the televangelist of a later day.

We can assume Sarason's involvement in the creation of Windrip's fifteen points, if indeed they were his and not Bishop Paul Peter Prang's, who claims they were stolen from him. The most attractive of the fifteen points is the promise to give each family $5000. Other points include the disenfranchisement of the Negroes, the return of women to their "incomparably sacred duties" (63), relegating Congress to advisory status, stripping the Supreme Court of its power to declare laws unconstitutional, raising Windrip's private army of Minute Men to full status equal to the regular army, and restoring veterans' bonuses. One result of the promised $5000 is a comic scene in the Fort Beulah hardware store jammed with locals placing orders against that expectation—which of course is never fulfilled.

Windrip's ambitions go beyond his fifteen points. They extend to the remapping and renaming of the entire country. States are divided into eight provinces. Fort Beulah is assigned to the Northeastern Province; provinces are divided into numbered districts and districts into lettered counties, which are further subdivided into townships and cities. Only townships and cities retain their old names, although rumors say they will be replaced by letters and numbers. Doremus now lives in Northeastern Province, District 5, County 13, Township of Beulah. The loss of state identity is more lamented than the castration of Congress and the Supreme Court, but most lamented is the failure to deliver the promised $5000. Universities fare as badly as the legislatures and the judiciary. The old ones disappear; the country now has only eight, one per province. The University of the Northeastern Province, for example, supplants Harvard, Radcliffe, Boston

It Can't Happen Here (1935)

University, and Brown (208). All universities have the same offerings, and undergraduate terms are shortened to two years.

Windrip holds power for two years before he is ousted by Sarason, who proclaims himself president, while Windrip is permitted to escape and live in Paris on his numbered accounts. The next palace coup assassinates Sarason, who failed to watch his back. His male-centered, luxurious lifestyle (modeled on some of Hitler's followers) is succeeded by an austere, puritanical regime. Sarason had arranged for others to be purged, like Bishop Prang of the Methodist Episcopal Church who was Windrip's only serious competitor. Prang had a weekly radio program, like Father Coughlin on whom he is modeled, and, together with his League of Frightened Men, a following of millions. He doesn't get far after confronting Windrip with his theft, even when his followers march on Washington. They are deflected and, soon after being reported suffering from a nervous breakdown, Prang is removed to St. Elizabeth's Hospital and never heard from again.[4]

---

[4] Bishop Morehouse in *The Iron Heel* suffers the same fate as does First Lady Anne Morrow Lindbergh for a spell in *The Plot Against* America. Mental illness continues as a way to dispose of political opponents in parts of the world.

It Can Happen Here

Doremus Jessup isn't mad, only "the prime eccentric of Fort Beulah" (9). He is unusual in other ways. Few fictional protagonists are sixty and the father of three grown children. Not the assertively virile Ernest of *The Iron Heel*, nor the seven-year-old Philip of *The Plot Against America*. Being eccentric in Fort Beulah means being liberal as Doremus defines that persuasion. "Brought up to revere the Abolitionists" (117), he reveres them still, but can wonder if other men could have done the job better. Able to undercut every point of view, even the most uncontested, he can, for example, question whether it was "such a desirable thing for the Thirteen Colonies to have cut themselves off from Great Britain" (116). He wonders whether his country has developed an individualism any greater than the Canadians or the Australians (116), whether we could have managed abolition better, or why we "jump at the sting of a gnat like Debs, and blandly swallow a camel like Windrip" (116). Or why utopias fail, like Robert Owens's Harmony Hall, or Brook Farm or Upton Sinclair's Helicon Hall. Doremus is, of course, highly critical of Communism, which is too theocratic and slavishly adoring of Russia. When he attempts to join forces with the Communists in their resistance to Corpoism, both sides discover they are not made for each other. Yet Doremus supported the recognition of Russia in the 1920s and labor radicals like Tom Mooney. These are the stances that define

It Can't Happen Here (1935)

liberalism for him and make him an eccentric in Fort Beulah. And eccentricity is close enough to madness to be tolerated—until Corpoism.

Doremus has a conventional wife who at least once surprises us with wit and wisdom, as when she remarks that Windrip sounds like a combination of Norman Thomas and Calvin Coolidge. Otherwise, Emma's "pliantly pious facade" (120) and shallow inner life make her an irrelevant presence under Corpoism. Doremus's son, who supports the Corpos, easily rises in their hierarchy. His two daughters stand with the father. After Mary's husband is summarily shot, "homicidal hate" (269) drives her, which she nurtures until she can exact her remarkable revenge. She joins the Corpos, learns to fly, and ultimately gets her target but dies in the effort. Ironically, she is considered a hero and receives a military funeral. Sissy, the youngest, gathers information for the Underground about the powerful, Corpo who was once the family handyman. The plot details are complicated, but Sissy's efforts lead to the Corpo's imprisonment and assassination by his fellow inmates.

Mary and Sissy are as remarkable as Lorinda in their different ways. They make a strong triumvirate. Lorinda Pike, who spoke out at the Rotary dinner, is known, according to Doremus, as "the local female crank, the suffragist, the pacifist" (123). Doremus breaks his silence after the murder of two professors at Isaiah College, one Jewish and one German-born. Those murders precipitate his scathing editorial against the Corpos, which he is advised not to print. Only Lorinda says to do it: "He had suddenly, from Lorinda, the resoluteness he had sought in church" (122). Life under Corpo rule makes her "fierce ... and vibrant" (203) and single-minded. Neither he nor Lorinda ever raises the question of leaving Emma. They take their current arrangement for granted, one considered acceptable by some but certainly sexist by feminists. It does give Lorinda the independence to act on her own, which she does when the Corpos confiscate her boardinghouse business. She gets restive under Corpo life and leaves, eventually for Canada, where she works against the Corpo regime. She is the one who arranges Doremus's escape from the Trianon concentration camp. Even when the two can arrange a life together, they go separate ways appropriate to their differing roles as agents of change. Lorinda may well owe something to Dorothy Thompson as well as to the fictional figure of Zenobia in *The Blithedale Romance*. Other analogues to Hawthorne's novel about Brook Farm are striking. Like Miles Coverdale, Doremus has his approximate Phyllis and Zenobia, the passive and the active female. It's as though, less directly than Hawthorne, Lewis is considering "the fundamental importance of the relation of the sexes" in utopia and the "real" world (Jones 220). Lorinda takes a still-radical feminist stance when she argues that she can never be "'free to love'" until the world's chains are gone. When Doremus responds that that time will never come, Lorinda returns, "'Then I shall never be free to love'" (274).

The last half of the novel is most effective. It concentrates on the Fort Beulah naysayers and forgoes the comic extravagance lavished on the Corpo hierarchy. Like Doremus, the naysayers end up in the town concentration camp, called Trianon, after the girls' school it once was. Its name and that of Fort Beulah are worth a detour. Trianon is from the small chateau built by Louis XIV for Mme. De Pompadour, his mistress. Calling a concentration camp by the name of a chateau meant for a mistress makes an appropriately grotesque contrast. The contrast between the exotic Trianon and Beulah's biblical origin is also extreme. The name *Beulah* is suitable in a New England whose European colonists were steeped in the Bible. It appears in Isaiah 62:4 and has come to mean a blessed place. The name of Doremus's college, Isaiah College, underscores the biblical source and indirectly alludes to that brave new world European colonists thought they had found. There is only one bucolic passage in the entire novel. It occurs when the Jessup family picnics in "the paradise of Beulah valley" (37). (Hawthornes's *Blithedale* is, of course, another name for the "happy valley.") That "paradise" seems compromised when the town is called a Fort, and its legions are not heavenly.

To present an effectively chilling portrait of concentration camp life in 1935 is an accomplishment. There were no camps yet in Hitler Germany. Today the details of camp life are well known—the physical brutality, the psychological strains, and the mass murders (the murders are not yet mass in Lewis) became fully known after the war in Europe ended in 1945. When Doremus is taken to Trianon, he is subjected to castor-oil treatments, interrogations, and beatings, which hospitalize him for over a month. Other inmates scream, go truly mad, and hang themselves. The waiting is intolerable. Everyone dreams only of escape and food and contends with the daily increase in stench, lice, and rats. Thoughts of home quite recede from the forefront of Doremus's mind. The disappearing self is the only reality.

Doremus is one of the lucky ones, of course. The New Underground[5] arranges his escape to

---

[5] The name is a bow to the Civil War Underground Railroad, which carried slaves to freedom.

It Can't Happen Here (1935)

Canada and his final transformation into a spy for them in Minnesota, his creator's home state. A traveling salesman of farm machinery with a new name, alone, without Lorinda, without Emma, without anyone he knows, Doremus has only the comfort of a book suitable to his sense of irony, Spengler's *Decline of the West*. His new identity is not physically as transforming as Avis's in *The Iron Heel*, but it is thorough enough. Lewis is not as obsessive as London in his use of identity change as a necessity of underground life, but perhaps London helped him become aware of the isolation and unrootedness of that life.

Doremus claims not to be an activist, but as a newspaper editor, he has had to be one. He does, for example, publish his attack on the regime, for which he is forced out; he serves as the editor of the local underground newspaper, and ends, like Avis, as a spy in his own country. These are activist pursuits, which belie Doremus's claims to be otherwise. This discrepancy may relate to what one critic calls Lewis's "double consciousness." That double consciousness governs the novel and is immediately on display in the novel's title, which says one thing and means its opposite (McLaughlin). Doremus has complicated and often conflicting beliefs, which suit his version of liberalism and may qualify as a kind of desirable double consciousness.

It Can Happen Here

Lewis's own political positions are interesting in this regard. As a boy of thirteen, he tried to enlist in the Spanish American War. That effort at thirteen is not, of course a sign of lasting allegiance. As a young man, Lewis joined the Socialist Party[6] for over a year and worked briefly as a janitor at Upton Sinclair's Helicon Hall, a time we can regard as his Brook Farm submersion. These are signs that Lewis could once entertain great social change. His connection to Jack London as a man and writer shows Socialist leanings. His 1914 essay title, "The Passing of Capitalism," could have been coined by Jack London. One of his letters to London is signed "Yours for the Revolution" (Schorer 170). After his death, however, Dorothy Thompson describes Lewis as "apolitical," or, "insofar as his social ideas were articulate and consistent, he was an old-fashioned populist American radical" (Thompson 42). This Lewis sounds a lot like Doremus in his often quoted credo:

I am convinced that everything that is worth while in the world has been accomplished by the free, inquiring, critical spirit, and that the preservation of this spirit is more important that any social system whatever (357).

---

[6] Like London's, his socialism was heavily influenced by H. G. Wells. Lewis named his first son Wells.

It Can't Happen Here (1935)

These words are given to Doremus, but the novel's embarrassing last line belongs to the omniscient author, who should have resisted them: "And still Doremus goes on in the red sunrise, for a Doremus Jessup can never die" (381).

Lewis's early political ideas are not in evidence in *It Can't Happen Here*. Doremus joins the New Underground, led by Walt Trowbridge, a Republican, not because he agrees with it fully, but because it is the best game in town. Trowbridge wants restoration, not revolution. Whether or when that will happen the novel leaves open. Roth also chooses restoration. In his novel's present time, FDR is reelected to end the bizarre Lindbergh interregnum and return to history as we know it. Neither novel imagines a restructuring of society. Only Jack London is bold enough or committed enough or wrongheaded enough to project institutional change.

The Plot Against America
(2004)

At a time when many writers slow down or repeat themselves, Philip Roth published a remarkable group of novels of which *The Plot Against America* (2004) is one. He had already had a long prolific and enviable career. Then, at age sixty-two, *Sabbath's Theater* appeared, to astonish its readers with the irrepressible carnality and rage of its aging puppeteer protagonist. That novel turned out to be but the first of an outpouring of novels that is not yet over. Roth's late period has become, in one critic's words, "an off-the-charts phenomenon" (Fulford). *Sabbath's Theater* was followed by a trilogy: *American Pastoral* (1997), *I Married A Communist* (1998), and *The Human Stain* (2000). In these novels, Roth confronts the troubling facts of his America—the Vietnam war, anticommunism and racism. Sabbath's rage, it could be said, did not disappear but took on different shapes.

It Can Happen Here

In all his work, Roth has barely strayed from the Newark in which he was born and raised as a lower-middle-class Jew. Out of this apparently limited, unpromising background, he has created a universe as rich as William Faulkner's Oxford, Mississippi. But Oxford was equally unpromising until Faulkner showed us differently. Newark, New Jersey, and Oxford, Mississippi: these sites, the urban immigrant northeast and the southern rural, white and black, utterly unlike each other, with absurdly different pasts and presents, are yet both inescapably American. Each writer made obsolete older literary terms like *regional*, which implicitly meant limited or provincial.

After fully engaging with volatile unresolved national traumas like race and Viet Nam in these late novels, Roth took another kind of journey at age seventy-one. He created a national history that never was but could have been. In *The Plot Against America* (2004) Roth imagines that Charles Lindbergh defeats FDR in the 1940 presidential election. The novel seems a fitting companion to the works that preceded it. The Viet Nam war comes to Newark in *American Pastoral*. The title, *I Married a Communist*, suggests ironies about domestic communism not very satisfyingly fleshed out in the novel, while issues of race in *The Human Stain* develop with the depth and power of Roth's best fiction. These novels turn on, revise, or reimagine American

The Plot Against America (2004)

history. Even Roth's most casual reader knows how restless and constant is his immersion in the American present.

Roth was in new territory when he decided to undertake a novel that rewrites the historical past. And he knew it. In a discussion of the genesis of *The Plot Against America*, he refers to two earlier novels, *It Can't Happen Here* and *1984*, that imagine fascist futures. Sinclair Lewis and George Orwell, like Jack London (whom Roth does not mention), imagine future societal perversions. But Roth can find no novels that pervert the past.[1] He does not mention accounts of origin, like Eden, from which humanity has fallen away. In that fall away from perfection, humanity enters reality, or history. Prehistory is as much a tabula rasa as is future history. These blank states are of no interest to Roth. In his novel, recorded history becomes a kind of contrapuntal shadow text against which the counterfactual narrative works. This shadow text also gives the reader the pleasure of watching the familiar past reworked.

---

[1] Roth bypasses Philip Dick's *The Man in the High Castle* (1962). In that novel, Dick creates an alternative past in which the US has lost World War II and the victors, Japan and Germany, have divided the continent into two parts; Japan controls the western half and Germany, the eastern half.

It Can Happen Here

The motives behind the creation of an alternative past are the same as those that generate a present or future utopia or a dystopia. The writer plays Cassandra to his own time. Roth plays his Cassandra role through an unusually intimate, perhaps unique, plot structure, which presumably derives from a pressing need to deal with his own past. He locates his American dystopia in the years of his own childhood, which happen to coincide with twentieth-century catastrophes: the later depression years and the rise of Hitler and World War II. Roth personalizes his primary characters. They are the Roth family, and one Philip Roth is the narrator. Yet Roth publishes his work as fiction, not autobiography. The apparent lack of disguise is deceptive. Roth appears to be saying, "OK, here I am." But, of course, he is no more "here" than if his narrator's name were David Copperfield or Stephen Dedalus. His tactic unexpectedly enlarges rather than reduces the slippery and complicated relationship between life and art. Roth sees the writer as a performer, "not least when he dons the mask of the first person singular, maybe the best mask of all for a second self" (*Writers at Work*, 276).

However singular Roth's distortion of the past may be, that distortion asks the inevitable question, the one that historians resist and novelists can indulge. What if events had fallen out differently? What if the atomic bomb had not been dropped? What if John

The Plot Against America (2004)

Kennedy or Robert Kennedy had not been assassinated? Or Martin Luther King or Malcolm X? Roth's simple and powerful "what if" is, what if Lindbergh had run against FDR in 1940 and won?

In 1940, the country had barely emerged from the depression. Hitler's accession to power occurred in 1933, the very year Philip Roth was born. By 1940, Austria and most of Europe, including France, had fallen. The German word *blitzkreig* for lightning war to describe the rapidity of Hitler's extraordinary march across Europe had entered the English language. The major holdouts, Spain and Italy, were Hitler's allies, and the Soviet Union had signed a nonaggression pact with Germany. Less familiar to the larger American public but very familiar to the Jews of Newark and elsewhere was the escalating repression against Jews. History was intimate. It lived at home in present time. Philip's father Herman followed the news passionately through radio, newspaper, and the local newsreels-only theatre. The threat of Nazism saturated the Roth household. Britain had been at war since 1939, having kept its promise to declare war if Hitler invaded Poland. But the United States and the Roths were at peace.

Or appeared to be. Or were on the verge of not being so.

It Can Happen Here

The opening paragraph of the novel has only two sentences. The first one begins and ends with the word "Fear." In a few words it moves, like the novel itself, from simple "fear" to "perpetual fear." The title of the last chapter, "Perpetual Fear," takes us back to the opening line. Though fear is insisted upon, the word "memories" softens that fear because where there are memories there has been survival:

Fear presides over these memories, a perpetual fear (1).

The second sentence identifies the narrator-survivor as a Jewish boy living or having lived under the Lindbergh presidency.

The astonishingly simple first chapter moves from general fear to the young Philip's specific nightmare. In a dream, while running from a pursuer, loose pages fall from his treasured stamp album "at the very spot on the sidewalk where we regularly played 'I Declare War'" (42–3) in an unstated but obvious parody of the grown-up war play going on in Europe. In an earlier reference, Philip plays the game "incessantly" (37). In his dream Philip sees on his page of 1932 Washington Bicentennials the name Hitler where Washington's name should be. The facing page causes him to fall out of bed screaming. Printed across the face of his

The Plot Against America (2004)

beloved 1934 set of ten National Parks, "across everything in America that was the bluest and the greenest and the whitest," he sees a "black swastika" (43).

The black swastika that ends the chapter is as much imprinted on Philip's mind and heart as it is on his stamps. All the talk in the Roth household and the neighborhood, on the radio, in the newspapers and the newsreels, all the events that lead up to Lindbergh's nomination have been bombarding him "regularly" and "incessantly" to translate perfectly into the mutilation of Philip's stamp album. The transformation of Lindbergh, "the adored Lone Eagle, boyish and unspoiled" (29), into someone anti-Semitic and pro-Hitler is a related mutilation.

How Roth translates the fears that pervade the grown-up world around him into a personal nightmare appropriate to his seven-year-old Philip is the triumph of the novel. The seven-year-old Philip is not the only narrator. He is directed and modulated by the grown-up Philip, who is there from the beginning to tell us he is remembering the Philip he was at seven. The result is remarkably successful, to the point that the dual narrative by the two Philips appears to be a single narrative. In short, Roth "keeps his bi-focal vision in perfect focus" (Charles). He takes us, finally, as neither London nor Lewis does—to the novel as story rather than as political possibility. How young Philip sees his world and how he suffers and changes is where the novel's heart is.

The family members become memorable, as characters rarely are in political novels. They need some discussion. "We were a happy family in 1940" (3), the older Philip tells us, perhaps in wry revision of the "all happy families are alike" opening of *Anna Karenina*. The happiness of the Roth family is already slated to erode, as the "were" forewarns us. The family cohesion and sense of security will be seriously undermined and will never quite recover. In the Roth world, the men work hard and "the women work all the time" (3). The depression governs the shape of their lives. Bess has had to forgo becoming a teacher. Herman's ambitions are never described. He has finished grade school and is now a "foot-soldier" insurance salesman, but the family distinguishes itself from the newly arrived Jews across the river in New York City who wear skull caps and have accents and who come to the door to collect money for a homeland. Philip doesn't understand. The Roths "already had a homeland for three generations" (4): "Our homeland was America" (5) . Philip is so secular and so American, he thinks in Christian imagery. Family lore connects his mother's first pregnancy with Lindbergh's transatlantic flight, calling it a "global annunciation" (5) accompanying "the incarnation of her first child" (5). When he is nine, Sandy, who can draw anything, "a bike, a tree, a dog, a chair" (20), will commemorate this incarnation in one of his drawings. Philip is not presented as a writer-to-be. His distinctive passion is stamp collecting, which happens to connect him to FDR, the president and first philatelist of the land.

FDR functions as the living political Ur-father of the Roth happy family. Washington, Lincoln, and FDR make a democratic holy trinity for the Roth father. Herman's reverence for them and his America remain undimmed by his experience of anti-Semitism in Washington, DC, or his rejection of a promotion in nearby Union where he would be the only Jew and there is a flourishing German-American Bund whose members sport lapel buttons reading KEEP AMERICA OUT OF THE JEWISH WAR(177). The Herman who loves to vote and has never missed an election fits de Tocqueville's ironic observation that for Americans, the vote defines political action. Politically contentious Herman may be, but he is also a "rescuer and orphans were his specialty," (358) as Philip tells us. Herman rescues Alvin, who may be called a war casualty. That rescue is temporary. A casualty of Lindbergh America, the orphaned Seldon's "rescue" ends the novel.

Herman believes for a long time that his America will survive, while the more pragmatic Bess prepares for the family's flight to Canada. She takes a job and keeps it until there is enough money for the flight she urges and Herman refuses. But Herman does know when to back away, as he does from the job in Union and as he will later do when he resigns from MetLife to avoid resettlement in the American heartland under the auspices of the Office of American Absorption. "It's their country" (226). Bess realizes, far sooner than Herman. She manages the major crisis in the novel "like a combat officer" (336). Her daily heroism is exceptional, performing as she does "Each day in methodical opposition to life's unruly flux" (341). The word *heroism* is not misplaced for Bess nor is it, finally, for Herman. They are the heroes of the novel.

By the time Sandy returns from his summer on the Mawhinney tobacco farm in Kentucky, he finds his family not at all heroic and worse than ordinary. He defines his mother and father as paranoid ghetto Jews. When he calls his father worse than Hitler and wants to sit at the White House dinner with von Ribbentrop and the Jewish Quislings who are members of his own family, he has gone too far. He is forbidden ever again to participate in Lindbergh activities.

The Plot Against America (2004)

The slippage Philip laments—"My family was slipping away from me right along with my country" (114) —had in fact begun before Sandy's summer in Kentucky. It begins when Alvin, their orphan cousin, who enlisted in the Canadian army to fight Hitler, returns disillusioned, angry, and coping with the loss of his left leg. "The boy whom my father had single-handedly changed from a callow-good-for-nothing into the family's conscience" (52) reverts to what Herman considers his earlier self, although Philip is less harsh about what Alvin has become. Alvin marries the daughter of Pinball Philly and becomes, like his father-in-law, a slots king. He and Herman end in a violent fight that hospitalizes Herman and parallels the national violence, with Alvin screaming he did it for Herman, then spitting in his uncle's face.

Alvin is "the renegade on my father's side," and Evelyn "the maverick on my mother's side" (86). Evelyn leaves her left-wing life to follow the Rabbi Bengelsdorf, first as mistress, then as wife, in his outsize support for Lindbergh. That new loyalty leads Herman and Bess to abandon her, although she is thought of as an orphan. Aunt Evelyn is responsible for Sandy's summer in Kentucky and his invitation to the White House dinner for von Ribbentrop. The courtly, mellifluous South Carolinian Rabbi also functions as a convincing plot conduit to the White House. Bengelsdorf becomes the head of the Office of American Absorption and a confidante of First Lady Anne Morrow. Some consider him her Rasputin. He could also be called the Radio Rabbi, by analogy with Father Coughlin, known as the Radio Priest. Inevitably, Walter Winchell calls him what he is, the "ultra-civilized Jewish Quisling" (242). Alvin does Winchell one better with his, "'They slipped a gold ring through his big Jew nose, and now they can lead him anywhere'" (37). Bengelsdorf, who comes close to caricature, will meet the fate he deserves.

Philip's Uncle Monty is cruder than Alvin but as witty and on target when he describes the Rabbi as "'the pompous son of a bitch [who] knows everything—it's too bad he doesn't know anything else'" (35). Monty, a player in the wholesale produce business, will survive under any regime. He can buy anybody. When the FBI follows Alvin, Monty fires him. When an agent follows brother Herman, Monty bribes the agent to lay off, then takes the bribe out of Herman's pay. Alvin, Monty, and Bengelsdorf are antiphonal figures quite unlike Herman. Bengelsdorf is the only upper-class Jewish figure in the novel and the only Jewish Quisling. The older Philip uses Herman, Monty, and the rabbi to describe three responses to the Lindbergh regime: "My father chooses resistance, Rabbi Bengelsdorf chooses collaboration and Uncle Monty chooses himself" (359).

The Plot Against America (2004)

Finally, there is Seldon Wishnow, the Roths' downstairs neighbor, no kin, yet closer than kin—in fact, Philip's secret sharer, "his other self" (222). The attraction-repulsion in their relationship is a classic feature of the doubling phenomenon, uniquely transplanted here to a pair of nine-year olds. Seldon wears the same size clothing[3] and shadows Philip "doggedly"(221). He is bright; he can teach Philip to play chess, but he doesn't know how to throw a ball. Of course not. When Seldon saves Philip's life after he runs away in Seldon's stolen clothes, the two boys are "helplessly yoked" (239), to Philip's great annoyance. Philip acts to be rid of Seldon by appealing to Aunt Sylvia to send the Wishnows instead of the Roths to Kentucky. His intervention misfires. With both families slated for transfer to the "heartland," Herman quits his job to work for Monty and the Wishnows go alone. Mrs. Wishnow dies in the Louisville race riots, the only fatality in the Roth circle, leaving Philip at once guilt-ridden and fearful that Seldon will forever sit at the family dinner table. The guilt sequence is clear: Philip had sent Seldon's mother to Kentucky and her death. He had orphaned his secret sharer: "This devastation had been done by me" (337). Seldon, the last orphan

---

[3] Compare the atypically benign boy doubles in Mark Twain's *The Prince and the Pauper* (1881) whose exchange of clothes targets class distinction.

rescued by Herman, is the vehicle for Philip's fall from innocence.

Thirteen years after Lindbergh flew from New York to Paris, the event remains as vivid and glamorous for the Roth boys as it was for those who were there when. More than vivid and glamorous, the flight has become the stuff of legend. The older Philip later ranks the Spirit of St. Louis as "the most famous small plane in aviation history—the modern-day equivalent of Columbus's Santa Maria and the Pilgrims' Mayflower" (307). This glorification persists even after Lindbergh has become the evil antipode of Roosevelt. The boys adore him. Sandy hides his heroic portraits of Lindy and his plane, and Philip hides his commemorative stamps of the 1927 flight, lest their parents should find and destroy their treasures.

Lindy's mastery of the moment and the media is extraordinary. He turns up at the Republican convention at 3:15 a.m. to break a deadlock and be declared the party candidate by acclamation. He needs no campaign strategists, no reporters, no photographers, no speechwriters, and no focus groups to run his campaign. He conceives of his major strategy entirely on his own—to fly to every one of the forty-eight states in full flight gear for

The Plot Against America (2004)

a day. Counting on the anti-interventionist ethos, called isolationist, that followed World War I, he runs on the slogan, "Vote for Lindbergh or Vote for War." He wins easily. His administration doesn't become lethal until after he leaves the country, effectively abdicating, and his isolationist vice president Burton K. Wheeler takes over. The "Accords" he signs with Germany and Japan or the establishment of the Office of American Absorption, Just Folks, or Homestead 42 (surely grim analogues to the CCC and the WPA under FDR or the Patriot Act of George Bush the younger) seem benign by comparison with the martial law that is to follow.

Walter Winchell, the man who stands up to run against Lindbergh, is a wholly unlikely unheroic opponent out of the rackets world of Uncle Monty, Alvin, Pinball Philly, and other choicely named figures like Bullet Apfelbaum and Knuckles Kimmelman. A seriocomic figure indeed—but he has guts, and he is, after all, "America's best-known Jew after Einstein" (19). All Summit Avenue has its radios blaring as this loudest of loudmouth Jews in the land gives his weekly broadcast. Everyone takes to the streets to greet the announcement of his candidacy for president. Neither his "standard feverish patter" (263) nor his "gutter charm" turn his audience away. When placed beside Lindbergh,

It Can Happen Here

as Mayor LaGuardia will say in his funeral oration after Winchell's assassination in Louisville, Kentucky, "'Walter's vulgarity is something great and Lindbergh's decorum is hideous'"(305). To have Winchell's body lie in state in Pennsylvania Station is one of Roth's inspired seriocomic inventions. Never mind that Winchell became in later years a right-winger, as Roth's Appendix to recorded history tells us—or reminds us if we did know—he is in this alternate history, effectively vulgar, brave, and on the right side. Then Winchell is gunned down. For the first time in American history, a presidential candidate is assassinated. But it happens again when RFK is gunned down in 1968 (271). Roth cannot resist telling us this datum—which gives away the restoration that is to come.

The first race riots break out in Detroit, the home of Father Coughlin, Henry Ford (now in the Lindbergh cabinet), and Gerald L. K. Smith. (Could Roth also have been thinking of the race riots in Detroit during World War II by blacks? Blacks are almost invisible in the novel.) These figures represent the powerful strain of homegrown fascism. It did not need to be imported, as parties in power usually claim. Once ignited, the riots travel to other major cities. Only at this point, with pogroms in full swing, does the Weequahic section of Newark respond as a community by organizing a defense contingent, should riots come to it.

There is no political action in the novel, either before or during the Lindbergh administration. Herman votes, and Evelyn was once active in the leftist teachers' union. The left is effectively absent in a period when its strength was considered formidable. There is no organized opposition to Lindbergh. Nevertheless, the restoration takes place. The Roths are unlike the activist figures in the London and Lewis novels. They do not need to be. But surely the restoration to history as we know it could have been managed more convincingly. Roth, the overarching third voice who wrote the novel, simply lets it all go. Lindbergh flies off, not into the sunset, but eastward, "never to be seen again" (307). At that point, Roth cedes the narrative voice of the novel to the Newark Newsreel Archives. These Archives hastily wrap up the public events before the novel returns to the Roths in the final chapter. The major event in the final chapter, Seldon's rescue, is an event neither Philip the young nor Philip the adult could have known firsthand. The voice in that chapter, the voice of the author who put the entire narrative together, concludes the novel.

It Can Happen Here

Perhaps the novel's version of America endorsed by the three voices can partly explain the rude deus-ex-machina resolution Roth the author accepted for his novel. The Roth family visit to Washington, DC, an exceptional venture outside the security of Newark, defines that city's glory and risk. It is the best place to find the Roths' mythic America. In that journey, the Roths are more than tourists; they are pilgrims. They count on "American history, delineated in its most inspirational form, to protect us against Lindbergh" (58). Standing at the Lincoln Memorial with the Washington Monument behind them, the young Philip Roth takes in "the most beautiful panorama I'd ever seen, a patriotic paradise, the American Garden of Eden spread before us" (66). But in the same sentence, Philip describes his family as "expelled" from this Eden, referring to their expulsion from their hotel room as Jews. The contrast between Eden and expulsion undergirds the chapter. Twice Herman is called a "Loudmouth Jew," the phrase inscribed yet again in the title of the chapter. The seven-year-old Philip can gasp at the glory he sees, marvel that their guide bears the name of the twelfth president of the country, and delight in "the opportunity to watch someone eat who'd grown up in Indiana" (74). But the triple repetition of "Loudmouth Jew" and the family's expulsion from Eden comment forcefully on the

The Plot Against America (2004)

contradiction between official Washington and its living, flawed residents.

In a way, however, young Philip's storybook view of American history wins the day. The family had counted on "American history ... to protect us against Lindbergh," and perhaps that unconvincing abstraction, "American history," had, against all odds, indeed protected the Roths, for the restoration is precipitated almost in deus-ex-machina fashion by the intervention of Our Lady of the White House, as Anne Morrow Lindbergh is called. She sets off the chain of events that depose the "un-American" Lindbergh regime. The view of history is naive but credible in a seven-year-old, another reason the choice of so young a narrator makes such good sense.

The child's eye of the young Philip has another advantage. It leavens the darkness of the novel. Whether Philip tries to figure out how much a lost leg weighs or notices that Mr. Wishnow hangs in the closet "amid ... the galoshes" (168), the grimness of events is leavened by his child's eye. Roth has always been attracted to the seriocomic; as he puts it in an essay, "Sheer Playfulness and Deadly Seriousness are my closest friends" (111). His closest friends are abundantly on display in *Plot*, not least in his mastery of parody. Whether he is mimicking a *New York*

It Can Happen Here

Times editorial, Winchell, FDR, LaGuardia, or a *New York Daily News* headline like "NAZI BIGWIG WHITE HOUSE GUEST"(198), his touch is perfect. He is equally adept with gangster talk or with the highbrow pretentiousness of the Rabbi Bengelsdorf (198). There is a little book of parodies within the larger novel.

Of course, at least one other reason behind the restoration must be laid to Roth's strengths—they are focused on the Roth family, not on the hows and whys of effecting a restoration of history. Some critics do not even consider *Plot* a political novel (Saval, Yardley). Roth hasn't the same kind of political imagination we find in London or Lewis which many would claim is all to the good. But he walks away from his novel entirely. Lindbergh's flight away from it all suggests Roth's impatience to get history right side up and return to the lives of the Roths. The two year swerve away from recorded history in *Plot* and return to the lives of the Roths is finally an aberrant event, as the imagined futures in London and Lewis are not. In their novels, fascism is so successfully entrenched in power it will be overthrown only in a far, far future. London's conceit is that the novel he has written is found seven centuries later, when the good society has come to exist. Lewis's novel closes with the protagonist

The Plot Against America (2004)

active in an underground that has a long way to go to overthrow fascism. London's protagonists did not want restoration but revolution. Although so unlike nineteenth-century utopias in so many respects, *The Iron Heel* is like them in wanting some form of socialist change.

History has at least three faces in Roth's novel. One is the formidable public record of public events. That history is "harmless history" (114). It makes what has happened inevitable. The other history, the history we live, not the history we read about, is brilliantly described by the adult Philip as the "terror of the relentless unforeseen" (114). Roth captures in that phrase and in his book a kind of personal terror absent in London and Lewis. "The relentless unforeseen" has come upon the young Philip too early and too fully. He cries out finally against it: "I wanted nothing to do with history. I wanted to be a boy on the smallest scale possible. I wanted to be an orphan" (133). His father's definition of history takes in his anguish. He tries to explain that history "is everything that happens everywhere. Even here in Newark" (180). It can be writ small as well as large. Herman's history is the most capacious and the most human. Unexpectedly and inexorably, of course, one of "history's outsized intrusion[s]" (184) comes to afflict the Roths and their circle.

It Can Happen Here

The noun *America* appears frequently in Roth's novel after its debut in the title itself. There are no references to America in the London and Lewis novels that have special meaning, and certainly no link established between America and Eden. Roth establishes such a link so strongly that present-day America seems to coexist with that brave new world of the early European explorers, perhaps jogging us to notice that Newark was meant to be New Ark. London shows no interest in the American past, and the Lewis citations to Jeffersonian ideals are to a country only, not to a uniquely blessed entity that could support the case for American exceptionalism.

But Roth's America seems always paired with a dark side. Roth wisely does not close the novel with restoration. Restoration happens in the penultimate chapter, but brings no relief to the Roths. The final chapter backtracks to the harrowing rescue of Seldon from the "vast Christian unknown" (342), then concludes with Philip trying to take in the outsize adult consequences of his childhood transgression. Roth leaves his reader with young Philip alone in the darkness of his sin and guilt. His young protagonist, bereft of both his Edenic self and his "incomparable American childhood" (301), has grown old too soon. We are forced back to the beginning of the novel to Philip's nightmare of the swastika overlaid on his precious National Parks stamps except that his fear has become "perpetual"— "Even here in Newark."

Afterword

To talk about the dystopian novel means talking about ideas and the novel. That is difficult. Ideas are usually thought to serve fiction badly—yet fiction has ideas. Indeed, dystopias, like utopias, are predicated upon them. Critical works like the Manuels' two-volume *Utopian Thought in the Western World* or Jameson's *Archaeologies of the Future* go straight for the jugular of ideas and the novel without a problem. Literary critics usually strike at novels differently. One critic, for example, calls *It Can't Happen Here* "inferior as art but effective as propaganda" (Tanner 61). That bifurcation is familiar in literary criticism. Trotsky frames the division a little differently when he describes the form of *The Iron Heel* as "only an armor for social analysis and prognosis"(v). Blackmur and Trotsky are an unlikely pairing, but when Blackmur calls *It Can't Happen Here* "a weapon of the intellect rather than a novel" (108), he is essentially saying the same thing. Both are allowing for a wider way into the novels when they bypass the "inferior as art" approach. When Henry James applied his great phrase, "loose baggy monsters" (*Art* 84) to some novels, he meant it disparagingly, but it will serve positively to describe the novel as the most capacious of prose forms. It allows for the full and the fitted and all other shapes. The novel is not a prescriptive form.

Three very different writers were moved to write against a perceived national threat not from an invading army or ideology but from native fascist movements. They chose the American quadrennial presidential year as their locus. In both the Lewis and Roth novels, right-wing parties, led by Windrip in one and Lindbergh in the other, are elected, as was Hitler. In London the election of 1912 brings the Socialists and their allies to power. The Oligarchy begins its takeover by throwing a bomb in the House of Representatives. Once it acquires power, it retains it for centuries. Lewis's fascists are still in power when the novel ends. Only Roth optimistically has the Lindbergh forces deposed by an election after only two years in office. The elections of 1912, 1936, and 1940 center the political rebellions in each of the three novels.

The years 1936 and 1940 are kindred years. FDR was a winning candidate in both. For Lewis, 1936 is just a year away; for Roth, 1940 is a remembered year of his childhood. Both display the racism, the anti-Semitism, the severe economic dislocation, the labor struggles, and the threat of fascism abroad and at home common to the period. The year 1912 shows most of these features, but it is historically far from the consciousness of Lewis and Roth. Distinctive to London is a strong interest in social structure the other writers do not share. London alone has the " larger view of politics as a collective mode of action," which Howe misses in Henry James (150). However, London's protagonist, like London himself, was more a loner than a party member, one who distanced himself from the Socialists as naïve and incapable of effective political action.

The world of the early explorers is long gone in these novels. It was long gone for the narrator of *The Great Gatsby*, who imagines at the novel's end "the fresh green breast of the new world" that "flowered once for Dutch sailors' eyes." Neither London nor Lewis shares that vision of the American past. For them, America is not a place uniquely endowed either by nature or history. The pastoral world in Roth's novel, although barely present, is rich by comparison with pastoral in London and Lewis. Its small but powerfully reverberating place on Philip's National Parks stamps is not real. It is only a miniaturized reproduction of a preserved wilderness in the stamp album which Philip later loses along with his innocence. The Roths do have a garden, but it is not in the National Parks or in Avis and Ernest's "green country"[1] in California or in the Beulah valley in Vermont, where the Jessups picnic, but in the urban enclave of Washington, DC. The Roths venture forth from Newark only on exceptional occasions—young Philip to chase Christians and the family to check out Union, NJ as a place to live should Herman accept his job promotion or rescue Seldon from Kentucky. The pilgrimage to Washington is one of those exceptional journeys. It is indeed a pilgrimage to the holy city where the sainted Washington, Jefferson, and Lincoln preside over that "patriotic paradise, the American Garden of Eden" (66). That metaphoric garden may be all the pastoral the Roths inhabit, but it endorses allegiance to the idea of American promise even when realities contradict it.

The word *pastoral* is not one we expect to encounter in Roth. That makes its up-front place in the title of another Roth novel particularly startling and worth noting. *American Pastoral* gives pastoral unusual presence in a novel describing the painful deterioration of family and city. However ironically and

---
[1] In 1984, Winston Smith calls his green idyll "the Golden Country."

deliberately misapplied, the word shows the lingering hold the idea of pastoral has on the American psyche in a world essentially denuded of it. Although pastoral has become metaphor, its absence is a presence in *The Plot Against America*, a novel whose major place names, New-ark and Weequahic, assert the consequential strains of American origins.

The Roth urban pastoral becomes repressive when native fascists win Congress and the White House in *The Plot Against America*, as they do in *It Can't Happen Here*. Roth keeps repression localized to the Roths, their extended family, and the Wishnows; Lewis extends it to the community of Beulah, London, to the city of Chicago, where repression and murder explode into apocalypse. News reports enlarge terror nationally in all three dystopias which postulate the inconceivable: an American reign of terror. But no reign of terror on the scale imagined by these novelists has happened here. Fascism did not come to power in this country in the twentieth century, but the potential was and still is there. "The unpredictability that is history" (Roth, *NYTBR*) forbids our assuming that "a realization ... of a certain potential in American political life" (Coetzee) can never happen.

Appendix

George Orwell Reads Jack London: *The Iron Heel* (1908) and *1984* (1949)

Orwell reviewed a new edition of *The Iron Heel* in 1940 under the title "Prophecies of Fascism." He found the novel weak as a novel but politically astute, particularly in London's conviction that the transition from capitalism to socialism would not "be automatic or easy" (30) because of the strength of the capitalist class (30). Orwell did not believe that that class would "'perish of its own contradictions' like a flower dying at the end of a season," as much socialist theory would have it. It would instead counterattack, "and the resulting struggle would be the most bloody and unscrupulous the world had ever seen" (30). London concentrates on that struggle which ends with the victory of the Oligarchy, the proto-fascist elite of his novel. Orwell, in *1984,* is more interested in how his ruling elite, the Brotherhood, maintains power.

Orwell and London share a similar view of successful ruling class traits.[1] Orwell describes such a class as having a "strict morality [and] a quasi-religious belief in itself, a mystique" (31). Such elites, "neither idlers or sensualists ... can only maintain their position while they honestly believe that civilization depends on themselves alone" (31). These are Orwell's words. London's "active rich" (56) are similar: "They, as a class, believed that they alone maintained civilisation" (190). His narrator claims that she "cannot lay too great stress upon the high ethical righteousness of the whole oligarch class. This has been the strength of the Iron Heel, and too many of the comrades have been slow to realise it.... The great driving force of the oligarchs is the belief that they are doing right.... The point is that the strength of the Oligarchy today lies in its satisfied conception of its own righteousness" (191).

---

[1] Max Lerner, whose introduction to *The Iron Heel* I located in 2012, is the only critic I know to have observed the similarity between the two ideological opposites, the Oligarchy and the Brotherhood. His observation is especially astute since it was apparently made without his knowledge of Orwell's review of *The Iron Heel*.

Appendix

The Brotherhood shares with the Oligarchs a strong "sense of righteousness" that is likewise their "strength"(191). Revolutionaries are characteristically credited with rectitude and a sense of mission. The ruling classes are not. Like London, Orwell can accept the daring proposition that the Oligarchs are, "in a different way, just as brave, able and devoted as the revolutionaries who oppose them" (31).

Perhaps the kindred righteousness of the Oligarchs and the Revolutionaries made it possible for Orwell to turn them around or to combine the tactics of the one with the ideology of the other. In *1984*, the Brotherhood, composed of those who were once Revolutionaries, has become like the Oligarchy. It continues to carry a name that suggests a socialist ethos, although it has, in reality, betrayed the socialist dream. There are no ideals behind the Oligarchy and the Brotherhood. Both wish only to perpetuate their power.

London's conception of a self-perpetuating, austere, well-trained ruling class may well have influenced Orwell's creation of the Brotherhood whose rule appears to be "forever." Neither writer could credit a pleasure-seeking society like the one in *Brave New World* (1936), which Orwell disparagingly describes as a "world ... turned into a Riviera hotel"(31). Orwell postulates that "because of his own streak of savagery, London could grasp" what many on the left could not: "that hedonistic societies do not endure" (30). Nor were many on the left as clear-sighted as London and Orwell about the characteristics required of ruling parties, be they right or left. In 1940, Orwell had not yet begun to work on *1984*. When he did, *The Iron Heel* was one of the works that fed his imagination, as has not yet been but needs to be recognized.[2]

Surely the most indelible image in Orwell's novel owes more than a little to *The Iron Heel*. O'Brien's grim image of his party's rule in *1984* as "a boot stamping on the human face forever" is all too like an iron heel and, more specifically, like the capitalist Wickson's threat in London's novel that "We shall grind you revolutionists down under our heel and we shall walk upon your faces" (63). Orwell strengthens Wickson's threat by changing *walk* to *stamping* and *heel* to *boot*, a word at once more military and more British.

The image becomes a defining one for Wickson's exercise of power. It is used several times more.

---

[2] Orwell read *The People of the Abyss* as a teenager. It stayed with him and influenced his first book, *Down and Out in Paris and London* (1933), as well as *The Road to Wigan Pier* (1937). Like London, Orwell went disguised among the London poor. See Shelden (62,121).

Appendix

Ernest, the Socialist hero, predicts that "'the Iron Heel will walk upon our faces'" (97). His father-in-law, John Cunningham, echoes his prediction: "'The Oligarchy is about to tread upon our faces'" (98). He quotes Wickson: "'I [Wickson] told him [Ernest] that we would walk upon the faces of the working class–well watch out for your face'" (98). Then, as an early victim of the Oligarchy, Cunningham reports: "'They have already walked upon my face'" (132).

2008

References

PRIMARY WORKS

London, Jack. *The Abysmal Brute.* New York: Century, 1913.

———. "How I Became a Socialist" (1903). *London's Essays of Revolt.* Ed. Leonard D. Abbott. New York: Vanguard, 1926. 57–61.

———. *The Iron Heel.* (1908). Westport, Conn.: Lawrence Hill, 1980.

———. *People of the Abyss* (1903). New York: Macmillan, 1904.

Lewis, Sinclair. *It Can't Happen Here* (1935). New York: Signet, 1970.

———. "Nobel Lecture, The American Fear of Literature." December 17, 1930. *Nobel Lectures, Literature 1901 –1967*. Ed. Horst Frenz. Amsterdam: Elsevier, 1969.

———. "The Passing of Capitalism" (1914). *A Sinclair Lewis Reader: The Man From Main Street*. Eds. Harry E. Maule and Melville T. Cane. New York: Random House, 1953. 327 –339.

Roth, Philip. *The Plot Against America*. (2004). New York: Vintage, 2005.

———. "The Story Behind *The Plot Against America*." *New York Times Book Review*. September 19, 2004.

———. "Philip Roth." *Writers at Work*. Interviewed by Hermione Lee. London: Secker & Warburg, 1986. 267 –298.

SECONDARY WORKS

Auerbach, Jonathan. *Male Call: Becoming Jack London*. Durham: Duke UP, 1966.

Audubon, John James. *The Birds of North America*. 1827 –1839.

References

Bailyn, Bernard. *The Barbarous Years: The Peopling of British North America 1600-1675*. New York: Knopf, 2012.

Bartram, William. *Travels*. 1791, 1792.

Bellamy, Edward. *Looking Backward, 2000-1887*. 1888.

Beauchamp, Gorman. "Jack London's Utopian Dystopia and Dystopian Utopia." Ed. Kenneth A. Roemer. *America 4as Utopia*. New York: Burt Franklin, 1981. 91–107.

Blackmur, Richard P. "Utopia: or Uncle Tom's Cabin" (1935). *Sinclair Lewis*. Ed. Mark Schorer. Englewood Cliffs: Prentice Hall, 1962. 108–110.

Blotner, Joseph. *The Modern American Political Novel*. Austin: Texas UP, 1966.

Bourne, Randolph. "The State" (1919). *War and the Intellectuals*. Ed. Carl Resek. New York: Harper, 1964. 65–104.

Brooks, Van Wyck. *The Confident Years: 1880–1915*. New York: Dutton, 1952.

_____. *The Early Years: 1908–1921*. Ed. Claire Sprague. New York: Harper, 1968. rev.ed. Boston: Northeastern, 1993.

Charles, Ron. "Lucky Lindy, Unfortunate Jews." *Christian Science Monitor*. Sept. 28, 2004.

Cantwell, Robert. "Sinclair Lewis" (1936). *Sinclair Lewis*. Ed. Mark Schorer. Englewood Cliffs: Prentice Hall, 1962. 111–118.

Coard, Robert T. "Jack London's Influence on Sinclair Lewis." *Sinclair Lewis at 100: Papers Presented at a Centennial Conference*. Ed. Michael Connaughton. St.Cloud: St. Cloud State University, 1985. 157-170.

Coetzee, J.M. "What Philip Knew." *New York Review of Books*. 51(Nov. 8, 2004).

Cowley, Malcolm. *After the Genteel Tradition*. New York: Norton, 1937.

Dick, Philip K. *The Man in the High Castle*. New York: Putnam, 1962.

Eagleton, Terry. "Utopia and its Opposites." *Necessary and Unnecessary Utopias: Socialist Register 2000*. Near Woodbridge, Suffolk: Merlin Press/ Monthly Review Press, 1999. Ed. Leo Panitch and Colin Leys. 31-40.

References

Franklin, H. Bruce. "Introduction." Jack London. *The Iron Heel* (1908). Westport, CT: Lawrence Hill, 1980. ii –vi.

Frye, Northrup. 1957. *Anatomy of Criticism.* Princeton: Princeton UP, 1957, 1971.

Fulford, Robert. "'There are no second acts': Philip Roth Proves Scott Fitzgerald's Maxim Wrong." *The National Post.* 28 September 2004.

Hawthorne, Nathaniel. *The Blithedale Romance.* 1852.

Hicks, Granville. *The Great Tradition.* New York: Macmillan, 1933.

Howe, Irving. *Politics and the Novel.* New York: Meridian, 1957.

Huxley, Aldous. *Brave New World* (1932). New York: Harper & Row, 1969.

Jacoby, Russell. *Picture Imperfect: Utopian Thought for an Anti-Utopian Age.* New York: Columbia UP, 2005.

James, Henry. "Preface to *The Tragic Muse.*" *The Art of the Novel.* Ed. R.P. Blackmur. New York: Scribner's: 1934. 79 –97.

Jones, James T. "A Middle Class Utopia: Lewis's *It Can't Happen Here.*" *Sinclair Lewis at 100.* Ed. Michael Connaughton. St. Cloud: St. Cloud State U: Minnesota UP, 1985. 213-225.

Josephson, Matthew. *The Robber Barons.* New York: Harcourt Brace Jovanovich, 1934.

Kolko, Gabriel. *Main Currents in Modern American History.* New York: Pantheon, 1976, 1984.

Labor, Earl. *Jack London.* New York: Twayne, 1974.

Lerner, Max. "Introduction." Jack London. *The Iron Heel* (1908). New York: Sagamore Press, 1957. vii-xiii.

London, Charmian. *The Book of Jack London.* New York: Century, 1921.

Manuel, Frank E. and Fritzie P. Manuel. *Utopian Thought in the Western World.* Cambridge: Harvard UP, 1979.

Mannheim, Karl. *Ideology and Utopia.* (1929). New York: Columbia UP, 1955.

References

Marx, Leo. *The Machine in the Garden.* New York: Oxford UP, 1964.

McLaughlin, Robert L. "Mark Schorer: Dialogic Discourse and *It Can't Happen Here.*" *Sinclair Lewis: New Essays in Criticism.* Ed. James M. Hutchisson. Troy, NY: Whitson, 1997. 21-37.

Meisel, Perry. Introduction" (1993). Sinclair Lewis. *It Can't Happen Here* (1935). New York: Signet, 1970. 7-13.

Melville, Herman. "Hawthorne and His Mosses." *Literary World,* August 17 and 24, 1850.

Mencken, H. L. "Consolation" 1921. *Sinclair Lewis.* Ed. Mark Schorer. Englewood Cliffs: Prentice Hall, 1962. 17 –20.

_____. "Portrait of an American Citizen." 1922. *Sinclair Lewis.* Ed. Mark Schorer. Englewood Cliffs: Prentice Hall. 1962. 20 –22.

More, Thomas. *Utopia.* 1516.

Mumford, Lewis. *The Story of Utopias.* 1922. New York: Penguin, 1962.

Orwell, George. *1984* (1949). New York: Signet, 1950.

———. "Prophecies of Fascism." *Tribune* [London]. July 12, 1940 np. *My Country Right or Left :1940-1943. The Collected Essays, Journalism and Letters of*." III. Ed. Sonia Orwell and Ian Angus. New York: Harcourt, Brace and World, 1968. 30-33.

Parini, Jay. *Robert Frost: A Life.* New York: Henry Holt, 1949.

Rabelais, François. *Gargantua and Pantagruel.* 1532, 1534.

Rhodes, Richard. *John James Audobon: The Making of an American.* New York: Knopf, 2004.

Rideout, Walter. *The Political Novel in the United States, 1910 –1954.* New York: Hill & Wang, 1956.

Rourke, Constance. "Round Up" (1931). *Sinclair Lewis.* Ed. Mark Schorer. Englewood Cliffs: Prentice Hall, 1962. 29 –31.

Saval, Nikil. "*The Plot Against America* by Philip Roth." Logosjournal.com/issue_5.1.

References

Schorer, Mark, Ed. *Sinclair Lewis: A Collection of Critical Essays*. Englewood Cliffs: Prentice Hall, 1962.

_____. *Sinclair Lewis: An American Life*. New York: McGraw-Hill, 1961.

Shelden, Michael. *Orwell: The Authorized Biography*. New York: Harper Collins, 1991.

Simic, Charles. "The Nicest Boy in the World." *NYRB*. October 9, 2008, 4–8.

Skinner, B.F. "Utopia as an Experimental Culture." *America as Utopia*. Ed. Kenneth R. Roemer. New York: Burt Franklin, 1981. 28–42.

Stasz, Clarice. "Androgyny in the Novels of Jack London."*Western American Literature*. II(May 1976), 121-133.

Tanner, Stephen. "Sinclair Lewis and Fascism." *Studies in the Novel*. 22 (1990), 57–66.

Tavernier-Courbin, Jacqueline, Ed. *Critical Essays on Jack London*. Boston: G.K. Hall, 1983.

Thompson, Dorothy. "The Boy and Man from Sauk Centre." *Atlantic*.206 (November 1960), 31–48.

Trotsky, Leon. "Jack London's *The Iron Heel*" (1937). Jack London. *The Iron Heel*. Edinburgh: Rebel Inc.: Cannongate Books, 1999. v –viii.

Ward, Susan. "Ideology for the Masses: Jack London's *The Iron Heel*." *Critical Essays on Jack London*. Ed. Jacqueline Tavernier-Courbin. Boston: G.K. Hall, 1983. 166 –179.

Wells, H. G. *When the Sleeper Wakes* (1899) and *The Time Machine* (1895). New York: Harper & Row, 1980, 1984.

Whipple, T. K. "Sinclair Lewis." (1928). *Sinclair Lewis*. Ed. Mark Schorer. Englewood Cliffs: Prentice Hall, 1962. 71–83.

Whitman, Walt. "Democratic Vistas." 1867, 1868, 1871.

Williams, W. A. *The Tragedy of American Diplomacy*. New York: Norton, 1959.

Yardley, Jonathan. "Homeland Insecurity." *Washington Post*. October 3, 2004, BW02.

Zinn, Howard. *A People's History of the United States*. New York: Harper & Row, 1980, 1984.

Made in the USA
Monee, IL
10 November 2024

69776607R00075